recipes for a
healthy
heart

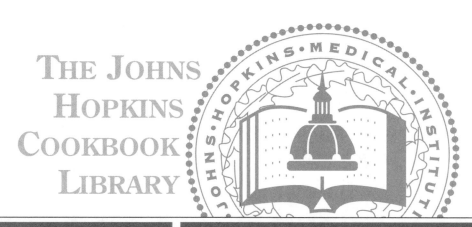

THE JOHNS HOPKINS COOKBOOK LIBRARY

recipes for a
healthy
heart

Medical Editor
SIMEON MARGOLIS, M.D., PH.D.

Nutrition Editor
LORA BROWN WILDER, Sc.D., M.S., R.D.

REBUS
NEW YORK

REBUS

This book is not intended as a substitute for the advice and expertise of a physician, pharmacist, or other health-care practitioner. Readers who suspect they may have specific medical problems should consult a physician about any suggestions made in this book.

Library of Congress Cataloging-in-Publication Data

Recipes for a healthy heart / Simeon Margolis, medical editor ; Lora Brown Wilder, nutrition editor
    p. cm. – (The Johns Hopkins cookbook library)
  Includes index.
  ISBN 0-929661-77-X
    1. Heart–Diseases–Diet therapy–Recipes. 2. Heart–Diseases–Prevention. I. Margolis, Simeon, 1931- II. Wilder, Lora Brown. III. Series.

RC684.D5 R43 2003
641.5'6311–dc21

                                                        2002036858

Printed in the United States of America
10 9 8 7 6 5 4 3 2 1

contents

Eating for Heart Health 6

    What to Eat and Why (chart) 8

Add These Foods to Your Diet 11

The Recipes

    A User's Guide 16

    Appetizers & Soups 18

    Fish, Meat & Poultry 37

    Meatless 82

    Side Dishes 99

    Desserts 122

    Breads & Breakfast 136

The Savvy Shopper 148

Leading Sources (nutrient charts) 151

    Recommended Intakes 154

Recipe Index 155

eating for heart health

Over the years, research has shown us that diet and exercise play an important role in the prevention of heart disease. And one of the primary goals of a heart-healthy diet is to obtain or maintain healthy cholesterol levels. Certain foods can help to reduce levels of artery-clogging LDL cholesterol as well as increase beneficial HDL cholesterol, which removes cholesterol from plaques in the walls of arteries. Because HDL protects against coronary heart disease (CHD), HDL cholesterol is often called the "good" cholesterol, while plaque-forming LDL cholesterol is referred to as the "bad" cholesterol.

In addition, keeping blood pressure under control and lowering triglycerides are key components of a heart-smart way of eating. Like cholesterol, triglycerides are a type of fat found in foods and are manufactured in the body. An elevated blood triglyceride level has recently been deemed an independent risk factor for CHD, especially in people with diabetes. And because obesity, too, is closely linked to elevated total cholesterol and triglyceride levels, and reduced HDL cholesterol, attaining or maintaining a healthy weight is another goal in CHD prevention.

Low-fat, nutrient-rich foods such as beans, whole grains, vegetables, and fruit should serve as the central focus of your meals, with meat used almost as a side dish. Consuming a mostly plant-based diet, along with low-fat dairy foods, fatty fish, poultry (with no skin), and small amounts of lean cuts of meat, will provide satisfying flavors and textures as well as all of the nutrients you need to help maintain lifelong health and cardiovascular well-being.

The recipes in this book offer a rich assortment of flavorful dishes that are both heart-healthy and easy to prepare. Health professionals advocate a heart-healthy diet for all individuals, regardless of heart disease risk. However, people with CHD, diabetes, high blood pressure, or high cholesterol should discuss changes in diet with a health professional, as specific dietary adjustments might be necessary.

maintain a healthy weight

Maintaining a healthy weight can help prevent the development of obesity-related conditions that increase the risk of CHD. Moreover, the distribution of body fat is an important predictor of health risk. Carrying extra weight in the abdomen (rather than in the hips, thighs, and buttocks) confers resistance to the actions of insulin, the hormone that regulates blood glucose. Insulin resistance leads to elevated blood levels of insulin, which are associated with high triglycerides, low HDL cholesterol, high blood pressure, and increased CHD risk—a constellation of conditions called "metabolic syndrome." A waist circumference

RECENT RESEARCH

NUTS HELP PREVENT HEART ATTACKS

According to data gathered from a recent large study, snacking on nuts may protect against fatal heart attacks caused by abnormal heart rhythms.

Researchers analyzed food frequency questionnaires from 21,454 male participants who were followed for up to 17 years in the United States Physicians' Health Study.

Compared with men who rarely or never consumed nuts, men who ate about 1 ounce of nuts more than twice a week were about 30% less likely to die from sudden death caused by heart rhythm abnormalities. Study authors speculate that alpha-linolenic acid, a type of omega-3 fatty acid found in small to moderate amounts in nuts, may protect against the heart rhythm problems that can lead to sudden death.

While this study adds to the findings of other studies that show a strong relationship between nut consumption and heart health, more research is required to understand the mechanisms of the heart-healthy properties of nuts.

Just don't go overboard with nuts since they are quite high in calories.

ARCHIVES OF INTERNAL MEDICINE
VOLUME 162, PAGE 1382
JUNE 24, 2002

of greater than 40 inches in men or 35 inches in women indicates abdominal obesity and a heightened risk for the development of metabolic syndrome. The good news is that abdominal fat is often the first to go with weight loss.

reduce harmful fats

Foods high in saturated fat can exacerbate existing CHD and contribute to its onset by raising LDL cholesterol levels. In general, foods high in saturated fat include animal fats and certain tropical oils such as palm and coconut oils and cocoa butter. Most animal foods are not only high in saturated fat, but also tend to be high in cholesterol. Exceptions to this are fish and shellfish, which, though high in cholesterol, are low in saturated fat. While it has less impact than saturated fat, dietary cholesterol can also raise blood cholesterol levels. Another kind of fat that elevates cholesterol levels is trans fatty acids (*see "What About Trans Fats?" on page 10*), which are found in an array of processed foods.

choose healthful fats

Of the three main types of dietary fat—saturated, monounsaturated, and poly-unsaturated—the last two are considered to be beneficial, heart-friendly fats, particularly when substituted for saturated fats. There is some evidence that a diet rich in monounsaturated fatty acids helps to improve blood levels of HDL cholesterol and triglycerides. Avocados, canola oil, nuts, olives, olive oil, and peanuts contain large amounts of monounsaturated fats.

Also useful in helping lower LDL cholesterol are polyunsaturated fatty acids such as omega-6 fatty acids (found in grains, seeds, and nuts, and in corn, safflower, sunflower, and soybean oils). Another type of polyunsaturated fatty acid linked to heart health are omega-3 fatty acids (plentiful in fatty fish and, to a lesser extent, canola oil, flaxseeds and flaxseed oil, soybean oil, and nuts). Because fish are rich in omega-3 fatty acids—especially fatty fish, such as salmon, mackerel, sardines, and tuna—the American Heart Association recommends that Americans consume fish twice a week. However, polyunsaturated fats, compared with mono-unsaturated fats, are more susceptible to damage from oxygen, a process that can promote the deposition of LDL cholesterol into plaques in artery walls.

reduce sodium

While we need sodium to help regulate blood pressure and maintain proper levels of body water and blood volume, too much sodium—a mineral found not only in table salt, but also in many processed foods, such as salad dressings and canned soups—can contribute to elevated blood pressure. Hypertension (high blood pressure) itself produces few, if any, symptoms, but is a primary risk factor for

WHAT TO EAT AND WHY

nutrient	food sources	health benefits
soluble fiber	apples, barley, beans, brown rice, carrots, oats, pears, prunes and other dried fruit	By interfering with the body's absorption of cholesterol, foods rich in soluble fiber are helpful in lowering LDL ("bad") cholesterol levels.
folate	asparagus, avocados, beans, beets, broccoli, chick-peas, fortified cereal, oranges and orange juice, lentils, soybeans, spinach, wheat germ	Folate is a B vitamin that helps reduce levels of homocysteine, an amino acid produced when the body metabolizes protein. Elevated homocysteine has been associated with increased risk for CHD. Another B vitamin, B_6, also helps to lower homocysteine levels. Speak to your doctor about taking a B-complex supplement.
soy protein	soybeans, soymilk, tempeh, tofu	When substituted for animal protein, soy protein helps to reduce LDL cholesterol.
complex carbohydrates	legumes (beans, peas), pasta, starchy vegetables (such as corn, potatoes, winter squash, sweet potatoes), and whole grains	Foods high in complex carbohydrates help contribute to feelings of fullness, which may help in weight control by preventing overeating.
omega-3 fatty acids	canola oil, flaxseeds and flaxseed oil, herring, mackerel, nuts, salmon, soybean oil, tuna, trout	Omega-3 fatty acids may help prevent cardiac arrhythmia and also reduce the formation of blood clots. Fatty fish are the best sources of omega-3s, because they have higher concentrations of this healthful fat.
monounsaturated fatty acids	avocados, canola oil, nuts, olives, olive oil, peanuts	When used in place of saturated fats in the diet, monounsaturated fatty acids help to lower LDL cholesterol levels.
potassium	apricots, bananas, citrus fruits, fish, green leafy vegetables, milk, nuts, potatoes, poultry, prune juice, tomato juice, whole grains, yogurt	People who consume optimum amounts of foods high in potassium generally have lower blood pressures than people whose potassium intake is low. Potassium also works in tandem with calcium and magnesium to maintain proper function of heart muscle.
antioxidants	apricots, berries, broccoli, carrots, citrus fruit, kale, kiwifruit, melons, nuts, peppers, spinach, sweet potatoes, tomatoes	While the benefits of antioxidants remain unproven, some health professionals believe that antioxidants may prevent free radicals from contributing to the oxidative damage linked to atherosclerosis.

heart disease as well as kidney failure and stroke. In general, reducing sodium in the diet lowers blood pressure in people who have hypertension, which in turn lowers their risk of CHD. Also, sodium reduction may help prevent hypertension from developing in some people whose blood pressure approaches hypertensive levels, especially older people and people with diabetes. Since it's impossible to know how much a person's blood pressure will be affected by too much sodium, it's a good idea for everyone to limit salt intake. Some tips for following a low-salt diet include going easy on the saltshaker, both at the table and during meal preparation; avoiding high-sodium foods, such as cured meats, canned vegetables, pickles, ketchup, soy sauce, and barbecue sauce; and looking for no-salt-added, low-sodium, or sodium-free labels when shopping.

get more of these nutrients

soluble fiber A diet rich in soluble fiber helps reduce LDL cholesterol without altering HDL cholesterol. Soluble fiber may also help regulate blood sugar in individuals with diabetes; and it may make you feel full—a major aid in weight-loss and calorie-restricted diets. Of the various types of soluble fiber, beta-glucan (found in oats, barley, and mushrooms) is thought to be particularly beneficial in lowering cholesterol. And pectin, another cholesterol-reducing soluble fiber, is found in apples, grapefruit, many other fruits, and some vegetables.

folate Foods containing high levels of the B vitamin folate may help to lower blood levels of homocysteine, a by-product of protein metabolism linked to CHD and stroke. Folate is now added to grain foods such as bread, flour, rice, pasta, and ready-to-eat breakfast cereals. Vitamin B_6 is also believed to play a role in

the grapefruit juice effect

Grapefruit juice contains a compound that may interfere with how certain medications are metabolized in the intestine. As a result, an increased amount of the medication can be absorbed into the blood. Higher blood levels of the medication can lead to side effects. A wide range of drugs may be affected by grapefruit juice, including cholesterol-lowering statins and calcium channel blockers. To play it safe, avoid drinking grapefruit juice within several hours of taking medication; and though there may not be enough juice in a single fruit to cause a problem, it is also prudent to avoid eating grapefruit when taking medication. Talk to your pharmacist or physician if you have concerns about the effects of grapefruit juice on your medications.

Recipes for a Healthy Heart

reducing homocysteine levels. To ensure that you are receiving adequate levels of the B vitamins folate, vitamin B_6, and vitamin B_{12}, speak to your physician about a B-complex supplement.

soy protein Replacing animal protein with soy protein helps to lower elevated blood cholesterol levels. The FDA has approved a health claim label for products containing soy protein: The label can say: "Diets low in saturated fat and cholesterol that include 25 grams of soy protein a day may reduce the risk of heart disease." To qualify, the product must contain at least 6.25 grams of soy protein per serving.

potassium Potassium is a mineral vital to numerous functions, including helping regulate the heartbeat. Too little dietary potassium may raise blood pressure, and conversely, increased dietary potassium may help lower blood pressure.

antioxidants Found in a wide range of fruits and vegetables, antioxidants such as vitamins C and E, and carotenoids (such as beta carotene, lutein, and lycopene) may help defend against free radical damage. Free radicals are created as a natural result of cellular reactions and are also generated from environmental sources such as cigarette smoke, radiation from sunlight, and pollution. While research has not proven that antioxidants protect against CHD, antioxidant-rich foods are extremely healthful and may offer protection against other diseases linked to free radical damage. Antioxidant supplements have been found to have little or no benefit, and may even be harmful to health.

what about trans fats?

While most people know they should avoid saturated fats, another type of fat, called trans fatty acids, has been linked to increased risk of CHD. Trans fats are formed in a process known as hydrogenation, which converts a liquid fat to one that is solid or semi-solid at room temperature. Trans fatty acids are even worse than saturated fats because they not only increase LDL cholesterol levels but they may reduce HDL cholesterol levels. About 25% of the trans fatty acids we consume occur naturally, such as in dairy products, beef, and pork. But the remainder are synthetic and are found in solid vegetable shortening, almost all margarines, storebought baked goods (such as cookies and crackers), and commercially prepared fried foods. The FDA recently issued a ruling that would require the amount of trans fats to be listed on food labels. For now, the only way to determine if a food contains trans fats is to look for "hydrogenated" or "partially hydrogenated" in the ingredient list.

add these foods to your diet

apples

what's in it Apples provide a good amount of both insoluble and soluble fiber, including a type of soluble fiber called pectin. Studies show that pectin and other types of soluble fiber help to lower blood cholesterol. A number of phytochemicals found in apples are under review for potential health benefits.

cook's notes: While the soluble fiber pectin is found in both cooked and uncooked apples, cooking will help to increase its bioavailability.

asparagus

what's in it Low in fat and calories, asparagus provides vitamin B_6, folate, vitamin C, niacin, riboflavin, beta carotene, and fiber. One cup of cooked asparagus will give you 263 mcg of folate, which is about 66% of the recommended daily intake for this important B vitamin.

cook's notes: To retain more of the water-soluble B vitamins, steam or microwave asparagus instead of boiling it.

avocados

what's in it Avocados are nutritious; they are rich in potassium, niacin, vitamin B_6, and folate. And though avocados are high in fat, their fat is mostly beneficial monounsaturated fat that, when substituted for saturated fat, helps to lower LDL cholesterol levels.

cook's notes: Avocado flesh turns brown rapidly when it's exposed to air, but sprinkling it with lemon or lime juice prevents discoloration.

bananas

what's in it Bananas provide large amounts of potassium, a mineral that protects against high blood pressure and is lost in the urine during treatment with certain medications. One banana contains 467 mg of potassium, which is about 16% of the daily recommended intake. Bananas are an excellent source of vitamin B_6 and the soluble fiber pectin, which helps lower LDL cholesterol levels.

barley

what's in it Barley is a rich source of complex carbohydrates and provides thiamin, niacin, vitamin B_6, iron, and zinc. Barley provides ample amounts of fiber, particularly beta glucan, a soluble fiber that helps to lower LDL cholesterol. In addition, 1 cup of cooked pearl barley will supply about 25% of the recommended daily intake (55 mcg) of the antioxidant mineral selenium.

cook's notes: Barley comes in various forms, including hulled, pearl (or pearled), and quick-cooking. The most nutritious of the three is hulled, because it still has its bran layer; but it can be difficult to find and takes longer to cook. Pearl barley and quick-cooking barley are nutritionally equal.

beans, dried

what's in it A nourishing, low-fat source of plant protein, dried beans are high in complex carbohydrates, fiber, B vitamins (especially folate), and minerals, such as potassium, magnesium, and selenium. Beans are particularly rich in cholesterol-lowering soluble fiber. And the insoluble fiber in dried beans helps to improve regularity by speeding the passage of food through the intestine. The ample fiber content of dried beans also bolsters weight-control efforts by contributing to a feeling of fullness.

cook's notes: The gas-causing culprits in beans are carbohydrates called oligosaccharides. Some research suggests that presoaking beans, and then discarding the soaking water before cooking them, will get rid of some of the oligosaccharides.

beets

what's in it Beets are a rich source of fiber, potassium, and folate. Notable for their sweet, earthy flavor, beets have the highest sugar content of any vegetable, while remaining very low in calories (1 cup of cooked beets has only 75 calories). And unlike many other vegetables, their full flavor is retained whether they are fresh or canned (which is the way most beets are sold in the United States). Fresh beets, though, have a characteristic flavor and a crisp texture that you don't find in canned versions; and some of the B vitamins in canned beets may leach out into the packing liquid.

cook's notes: The best way to cook beets is to bake or roast them with their skins on and their stem and root ends untrimmed. The reason for this is that if you peel beets, or cut into them at all, their deep purple color will leak out as they cook.

Recipes for a Healthy Heart

add these foods to your diet

blueberries

what's in it A rich source of antioxidants, blueberries are low in calories and rich in flavor. Blueberries also contain significant amounts of vitamin C, as well as pectin, a soluble fiber that helps lower cholesterol levels.

cook's notes: Eat blueberries fresh and uncooked to preserve their vitamin C, which is partly destroyed by heat.

broccoli

what's in it A high-fiber, nutrient-dense food, broccoli is a good source of folate, riboflavin, vitamin B$_6$, vitamin C, and potassium. Noted for its wealth of phytochemicals, broccoli is a leading source of sulforaphane, a compound that helps prevent cell damage associated with cancer, and other illnesses. Broccoli also contains beta carotene and lutein, two carotenoids with antioxidant properties.

cook's notes: To preserve broccoli's nutrients, cook it as briefly as possible: steam, microwave, or stir-fry it instead of boiling it. Raw broccoli has more vitamin C than cooked; however, cooking will make the carotenoids in the vegetable more bioavailable.

carrots

what's in it Carrots are an exceptional source of plant pigments called carotenoids, which are so named because they were first identified in carrots. Carrots are the leading source in the American diet of the antioxidant beta carotene. Along with beta carotene, carrots also supply alpha carotene and lutein, other carotenoids that have antioxidant properties. The carrots with the deepest color contain the most carotenoids.

cook's notes: Because carotenoids are fat-soluble nutrients, cooking carrots with a little bit of fat (preferably monounsaturated fat, such as canola or olive oil), or eating them with other sources of fat, makes the beta carotene more available for absorption by the body. Cooking also makes the soluble fiber in the carrots more bioavailable.

dairy

what's in it Low-fat (1%) or fat-free (also called skim) milk and yogurt provide high-quality protein, calcium, B vitamins (especially vitamin B12), and minerals, without the added saturated fat, which increases harmful LDL cholesterol (1% milk has a small amount of saturated fat but much less than whole milk). For the most calcium per cup, fat-free plain yogurt is the best, at 488 mg (about 40% of the recommended daily intake). After that, in descending order, are low-fat yogurt (448 mg), fat-free milk (352 mg), and 1% milk (300 mg), all excellent sources of calcium.

fish, fatty

what's in it All fish are an excellent source of lean protein, vitamins B$_{12}$, B$_{12}$, E, and niacin, as well as selenium and iron. And fatty fish such as salmon, mackerel, tuna, herring, and sardines are particularly notable for their rich supply of heart-healthy fats called omega-3 fatty acids. In fact, they are so beneficial for cardiovascular health that the American Heart Association recommends that people eat two servings of fatty fish a week to prevent heart disease. It is believed that omega-3 fatty acids help lower the risk of developing an irregular heart rhythm that can cause fatal heart attacks. These fats

may also help reduce blood clotting. Exactly how omega-3 fatty acids yield these benefits is under investigation. And while fatty fish do contain moderate amounts of dietary cholesterol, they are low in saturated fats, which are more of a health risk than dietary cholesterol. Canned salmon and sardines, with the bones, are also a good source of calcium.

cook's notes: Fish should be cooked in order to destroy parasites and potentially harmful microorganisms that are present in raw fish.

flaxseed

what's in it Flaxseed is an ancient seed that is undergoing a resurgence of popularity. The health benefits of this tiny seed are linked to a wide range of nutrients, including alpha-linolenic acid (ALA), one of the fatty acids essential for human growth and development. The body converts ALA into the same type of heart-healthy omega-3 fatty acids found in fish oil. Flaxseed is also high in potassium and phytochemicals called lignans, which are being studied for their potential to prevent hormone-related types of cancer. Generous quantities of both soluble and insoluble fiber are also present in flaxseed. The insoluble fiber helps to promote bowel regularity. A considerable amount of the soluble fiber in flaxseed is mucilage, a thick, sticky substance that may help to lower LDL cholesterol. The oil pressed from flaxseeds also contains ALA, but the fiber and lignans in the whole seeds are lost during processing.

cook's notes: Because flaxseeds are tiny and have a hard outer coating, they must be ground or thoroughly chewed; otherwise they can pass through the body undigested. You can use a coffee grinder to grind them. To preserve its alpha-linolenic acid and mild flavor, store flaxseed oil in the refrigerator and use it mostly in uncooked dishes such as salads.

fruit, dried

what's in it While each type of dried fruit differs in its nutritional makeup, they all abound in minerals and fiber, especially soluble fiber, which helps to lower cholesterol. These nutrient-dense snacks are high in carbohydrates and are a good source of potassium. In addition, apricots contain the antioxidant beta carotene. However, the drying process that concentrates the nutrients in dried fruit also concentrates their sugar content, which increases their calories. While one raisin doesn't have more calories than one grape, ounce for ounce, you'll be getting more calories. So while they are highly nutritious, it is a good idea not to go overboard with dried fruit, particularly if you need to watch your weight.

cook's notes: Cooking dried fruit helps make the soluble fiber more available to the body.

grains, whole

what's in it Whole-grain foods such as whole-grain breads, brown rice, and oatmeal, are high in fiber and provide complex carbohydrates, folate, riboflavin, thiamin, niacin, iron, zinc, magnesium, selenium, and vitamin E. Studies have shown that whole-grain foods help to lower the risk of type 2 diabetes and cardiovascular disease. Whole grains retain their bran (the fiber-rich outer layer of the grain) and the germ (the nutrient-dense inner

part), which provide nutrients and phytochemicals. Wheat germ, for example, offers folate, thiamin, magnesium, vitamin B_6, iron, selenium, vitamin E, zinc, and fiber. It is also rich in polyunsaturated fats. Wheat bran, the outer layer of the wheat kernel, provides fiber, B vitamins, protein, and iron. The Food Guide Pyramid recommends that adults eat 6 to 11 servings of grain foods daily; several of those servings should be whole grains. Look for products with "whole grain" or "100 percent whole wheat" at the top of the ingredient list to make sure you are buying whole-grain foods. High-fiber whole grains are heart-healthy and they are also helpful in weight loss.

cook's notes: Because the germ of whole grains contains oil, whole-grain products should be refrigerated to prevent them from turning rancid.

kale

what's in it One of the best sources of the antioxidant lutein, kale is low in calories and rich in vitamin B_6, vitamin C, and iron. A yellow pigment (the yellow is concealed by the chlorophyll in green leaves), lutein may help to protect the eyes against macular degeneration and cataracts. Other carotenoids found in kale are zeaxanthin and beta carotene. Because kale is a cruciferous vegetable, it is endowed with phytochemicals called sulforaphane and indoles that may prove to be instrumental in protecting against certain types of cancer.

cook's notes: Cook kale with a small amount of olive oil to enhance the bioavailability of the carotenoids beta carotene, lutein, and zeaxanthin.

kiwifruit

what's in it Kiwifruit provides a rich assortment of nutrients such as vitamin C, fiber, potassium, folate, and magnesium. Particularly noteworthy is its abundance of the carotenoid lutein, which is associated with a reduced risk of cataracts and macular degeneration. Furthermore, kiwifruit contains the antioxidant vitamin E—and unlike most other sources of vitamin E (such as vegetable oils and nuts), kiwifruit is low in fat and calories.

cook's notes: To preserve the vitamin C content in kiwifruit, it is best to eat the fruit uncooked. If you combine kiwifruit with meat, poultry, or fish (in a salad, for example), don't let the mixture sit too long before serving; kiwi's enzyme, actinidin, will begin to "tenderize" the animal protein and turn it mushy.

lentils

what's in it These little disk-shaped legumes are high in fiber, iron, thiamin, vitamin B_6, zinc, and folate. Plant protein and complex carbohydrates are also supplied by lentils, which have provided sustenance for people for thousands of years.

cook's notes: To protect the water-soluble vitamins folate and vitamin B_6, do not cook lentils in too much water; and if any cooking liquid needs to be drained off, try to use it in the recipe or save for soups or other dishes. Soluble fiber in lentils is made available as the lentils cook and the fiber dissolves. Eat foods high in vitamin C along with lentils to enhance iron absorption.

add these foods to your diet

nuts

what's in it As research accumulates, nuts have emerged as a nourishing, concentrated source of heart-healthy monounsaturated fatty acids, vitamins, and minerals. Most of the fat in nuts is unsaturated, which is more healthful than saturated fat. And their monounsaturated and polyunsaturated fats help lower blood cholesterol, especially when substituted for foods high in saturated fat, such as meat or cheese. Though the amino acid content of nuts isn't complete, it does nevertheless provide a high-quality plant protein. Each kind of nut has a different nutritional profile; for example, almonds are the richest source of vitamin E, Brazil nuts provide an exceptional amount of the antioxidant mineral selenium, and walnuts supply the most alpha-linolenic acid, which is believed to have heart-healthy properties. And because each type of nut is different, it is best to eat a variety of them. One of the best ways to prevent heart disease (and diabetes) is to control weight, so it should be noted that nuts are high in calories and should not be eaten in large quantities. If you do eat nuts, make sure to substitute them for other high-calorie foods and eat only in moderation.

cook's notes: Refrigerate or freeze nuts to prevent their oils from becoming rancid. To enhance the flavor of nuts before adding them to a dish, toast them in the oven or toaster oven for 5 to 10 minutes, or until fragrant.

oats

what's in it Oats are a whole grain food packed with valuable nutrients such as complex carbohydrates, protein, thiamin, iron, magnesium, selenium, and zinc. Their main claim to fame rests with their soluble fiber, which helps to lower LDL cholesterol levels. A cup of cooked oatmeal provides 4 g of fiber—16% of the total amount of fiber you should eat each day—and about half of that is soluble fiber. In fact, the FDA allows the labels on oat products to bear the statement that their soluble fiber, as part of a diet low in saturated fat and cholesterol, "may reduce the risk of heart disease." Studies also indicate that the fiber in oats may help control blood sugar and improve insulin sensitivity.

cook's notes: Overcooking oats may diminish the nutrient content.

oil, olive

what's in it An excellent source of the monounsaturated fatty acid oleic acid, olive oil also supplies vitamin E and certain phytochemicals. Studies indicate that monounsaturated fatty acids may reduce the oxidation of LDL, thus preventing its deposition into arterial plaques and reducing the risk of developing atherosclerosis. If you are watching your weight, you should keep in mind that while olive oil is a healthy, nutritious alternative to other fat sources, it is, nonetheless, high in calories and should be consumed in moderation.

cook's notes: To preserve flavor, store olive oil in an airtight container in the refrigerator or another cool, dark place, and use as soon as possible. Refrigerated olive oil will solidify, so you have to let it reach room temperature before it can be poured.

oranges

what's in it While most people tend to associate the benefits of oranges and their juice with vitamin C, they may not be aware that oranges are also a good source of folate, potassium, fiber, and thiamin. While 1 cup of orange juice supplies 91% of the suggested daily intake for vitamin C, the whole fruit offers the added benefit of more than 3 grams of fiber.

potatoes

what's in it Rich in complex carbohydrates, vitamin C, thiamin, iron, niacin, and fiber, potatoes also supply ample amounts of potassium. In addition, one large baked potato gives you almost 50% of the recommended daily intake of vitamin B_6. Low in calories, rich in nutrients, potatoes are an ideal food for people who are watching their weight.

cook's notes: Try to eat potatoes with the skin, where most of the iron and fiber are found. And if you boil potatoes, leave the skin on (even if you're peeling them after cooking) and try to reuse the cooking water, where many of the B vitamins wind up.

raspberries

what's in it Fragrant, delicate, and sweet, raspberries are low in calories and offer an impressive amount of vitamin C (1 cup provides 34% of the RDA) and a good amount of dietary fiber, much of it coming from the seeds.

cook's notes: Try to eat raspberries fresh, because cooking can destroy some of their vitamin C.

rice, brown

what's in it A nutritious whole grain, brown rice has only the outer hull removed, which means that it retains—along with its bran layer—thiamin, niacin, vitamin B_6, and small amounts of vitamin E. And because the bran is not milled away, brown rice provides four times more insoluble fiber than white rice.

soy foods

what's in it Low in saturated fat and containing no cholesterol, soy foods are a good source of thiamin, riboflavin, vitamin B_6, folate, fiber, iron, potassium, magnesium, protein and cholesterol-lowering plant sterols. And 1 cup of cooked soybeans will give you 22% of the RDA for vitamin E. Soy foods also contain phytochemicals called isoflavones, which may help relieve the hot flashes associated with menopause and possibly reduce the risk of certain hormone-related types of cancer. The nutritional value of each type of soy food depends on how it was processed. For example, while 1 cup of soymilk provides about 24 mg isoflavones, 1 cup of cooked soybeans will give you almost four times that amount (95 mg). Along with their impressive supply of phytochemicals, what also distinguishes soybeans and their derivatives from other legumes is that they are a complete source of protein because they contain all the amino acids necessary for the building and maintenance of human body tissues. And when substituted for animal protein in the diet, soy protein lowers total and LDL cholesterol and triglycerides without lowering HDL cholesterol. Researchers, however, are still unsure if it is the protein, the isoflavones, or

other phytochemicals in soy, that are responsible for soy's cardiovascular protection.

cook's notes: To preserve phytochemical content, minimize cooking time for tofu and miso by adding them late in the cooking process.

spinach

what's in it Highly nutritious, spinach has plentiful amounts of folate, magnesium, thiamin, riboflavin, vitamins B_6, C, and E, zinc, and the carotenoids beta carotene and lutein.

cook's notes: While raw spinach is a healthy addition to salads, to reap the full benefits from this leafy green, eat it cooked at least some of the time. Cooking helps to convert the protein, lutein, and beta carotene in spinach into more bioavailable forms. In addition, cooking or eating spinach with a small amount of heart-healthy fat such as olive oil will help the body absorb the carotenoids more efficiently.

strawberries

what's in it Strawberries are a good source of dietary fiber and vitamin C (1 cup supplies 96% of the RDA for this antioxidant vitamin).

cook's notes: It's best to eat strawberries fresh, because cooking can destroy some of their vitamin C.

sunflower seeds

what's in it Sunflower seeds furnish thiamin, vitamin B_6, folate, iron, magnesium, selenium, zinc, protein, and fiber, as well as linoleic acid, a type of essential fatty acid. Experimental studies indicate that linoleic acid may help lower the risk of stroke by reducing hypertension and platelet aggregation. Sunflower seeds

are also an exceptional source of the antioxidant vitamin E (1 oz will give you 95% of the RDA for this vitamin). While nutrient-dense sunflower seeds offer a concentrated array of vitamins and minerals, they are rather high in calories; if you are watching your weight, try to include them in your diet in moderation.

cook's notes: Keep sunflower seeds in the refrigerator so they don't turn rancid. Toasting sunflower seeds (in a dry skillet or in a toaster oven) brings out their flavor.

sweet potatoes

what's in it Among the most nutritious of vegetables, sweet potatoes are low in calories (about 143 calories per medium sweet potato) and high in nutrients such as vitamin B_6, vitamin C, iron, and potassium. Furthermore, one sweet potato provides over 25% of the RDA for vitamin E, which is highly unusual since most sources of this antioxidant vitamin tend to also be high in fat. The deep orange color of sweet potato flesh indicates that this vegetable contains carotenoids. In fact, one orange-fleshed sweet potato supplies just over 100% of the recommended intake for beta carotene (the darker the flesh of a sweet potato, the more beta carotene). These naturally sweet vegetables also contain other carotenoids such as lutein and zeaxanthin.

cook's notes: Baking or broiling enhances the bioavailability of carotenoids and sweetens the potato as its starches turn to sugar. Eaten with the skin, a baked sweet potato is an excellent fiber source.

recipes: a user's guide

focus on food, not numbers

The basic message, regardless of health concerns, is to eat a variety of foods, especially fruits, vegetables, and grains, with a minimum of fat (specifically saturated fat). If you follow these precepts, you probably will not have to concern yourself with fat and calorie calculations. (Note that your calorie needs are determined by a host of factors including body mass, how much you exercise on a regular basis, and such biological factors as metabolism and genetics.) However, if you are trying to keep track, the most important thing to understand is that you should be evaluating your intake not for an individual dish in a meal, and not even for the meal itself, but for a day's intake—and, ideally, for a week's intake.

nutrition analysis

Each recipe in this cookbook is accompanied by a nutritional analysis, including values for calories, total fat (with the amount of saturated fat in parenthesis), cholesterol, dietary fiber, carbohydrates, protein, and sodium. "Number crunchers" will want to use the actual values to determine their day's intake, but almost all of the recipes are designed to conform to sensible intakes of calories and fat (see "On the Menu," opposite page).

good source of

In the nutritional analysis for each recipe is a section called "good source of," which lists vitamins, minerals, and other healthful compounds. In order for a recipe to qualify as a "good source of" a nutrient, it must provide a certain percentage of the recommended daily intake for that nutrient (when there are different values for men and women—see the chart on page 154—our calculations are based on the higher of the two). In the case of a main-course dish, it must provide at least 25% of the recommended intake. Side dishes and desserts must provide between 10% and 20%, depending on their calories (the more calories a dish brings with it, the greater our expectation is for its nutrient content).

leading sources

In the back of the book, on pages 151-153, you'll find charts that list the "Leading Sources" of the nutrients featured in this book. A food makes it onto the chart by having at least 10% of the recommended intake for that nutrient (see the chart on page 154). Knowing which foods are especially high in important nutrients should help you when you are choosing foods to cook as side dishes, or even creating your own recipes.

spotlite recipes

In our "Spotlite" recipes, we focus on certain aspects of cooking that we think can make healthful eating more enjoyable or more efficient—or both. A "Spotlite" recipe can introduce a person who has an interesting contribution to make to healthful cooking, or it can focus on a healthy cooking technique, unusual ingredients, or time-saving cooking equipment. And sometimes we will take an old standby recipe and give it a health makeover. Here's what you'll find in these pages:

- **Chinese Dumplings** (page 22), an introduction to wonton skins.
- **Parmesan Fish Sticks** (page 40), an easy health makeover.
- **Salmon en Papillote** (page 49), learning a low-fat cooking technique.
- **Extra-Moist Turkey Loaf** (page 79), an interesting use of prune butter.

- **Quinoa with Fennel, Raisins & Parmesan** (*page 88*), the health benefits of an ancient grain.
- **Pumpkin Couscous Risotto** (*page 97*), discovering a quick-cooking pasta.
- **Root Vegetable & Apple Gratin** (*page 105*), from Michel Nischan, former Executive Chef of Heart*beat* restaurant in New York City.
- **Apple-Cranberry Sauce** (*page 128*), using a hand blender.
- **Buttermilk Waffles with Apple-Raisin Topping** (*page 136*), learning about flaxseed.

▶ homemade recipes

These are recipes for dishes that you might ordinarily buy premade, but whose nutritional profile you can improve by making them from scratch. Some of them can be put together on a weekend, when you have more time, and then stored in the refrigerator or freezer for future use. In this book, the homemade recipes are:

- **Broths** (*page 32*), including an unusually healthful chicken broth as well as a deeply flavored vegetable broth and a most interesting garlic broth.
- **Dipping Sauces** (*page 43*), simple ideas for turning a humdrum appetizer or main course into something special.
- **Marinades** (*page 56*), ways to improve the flavor of poultry, meat, and fish before grilling, broiling, baking, or roasting.
- **Turkey Meatballs** (*page 70*), low-fat meatballs to serve in soups, in pasta dishes, or on their own.
- **Breakfast Smoothies** (*page 140*), quick, tasty solutions for that important morning meal.

▶ off-the-shelf recipes

With these recipes we try to take advantage of convenient packaged foods without compromising the healthful nature of the dish. Since cooking from scratch takes time and fast food is often bad for your health, we've tried to find a satisfying middle ground.

▶ in the margins

On most recipe pages, you'll find tips that fall into one of the following categories:

F.Y.I. This is additional information on an ingredient in a dish or the nutrient content of a dish. For example, if the nutrition analysis tells you that the dish is a "good source of" folate, the F.Y.I. will explain which ingredients are providing the folate, and also remind you what folate is good for.

ON THE *Menu* If the fat or calories in an individual dish are a bit high, On the Menu will suggest other dishes that will create a well-rounded meal and also keep the overall fat percentage of that meal at a reasonable level. It's important to understand that a dish should fit into the context of a full meal and not be evaluated on its own.

KITCHEN *tip* Kitchen tips are, as the title suggests, information of value to the cook: how to shop for certain ingredients, short-cuts to make the recipe easier, or an explanation of a technique used in the recipe.

per ½ cup	
calories	121
total fat	0.8g
saturated fat	0.2g
cholesterol	0mg
dietary fiber	8g
carbohydrate	23g
protein	8g
sodium	308mg

good source of: fiber, folate, magnesium, potassium, thiamin, vitamin C

F.Y.I.

Rich in cholesterol-reducing soluble fiber, black beans are naturally low in saturated fat and are an excellent source of protein and folate. Folate is a B vitamin that helps to reduce levels of homocysteine, an amino acid associated with elevated risk of heart disease and stroke. Studies at the United States Department of Agriculture also show that darker colored beans such as black beans contain phytochemicals called flavonoids that may possess antioxidant potential.

Fat-Free Black Bean Dip

A wonderful appetizer dip with the unorthodox zing of fresh ginger. Though ½ cup of this dip has a little over 0.5 gram of fat, it's coming from the beans, cumin, and chili powder, making it primarily healthful unsaturated fat. Serve the dip with vegetable sticks, baked tortilla chips, or our Spicy Mexican Chips (*opposite page*).

2 cloves garlic, peeled
2 tablespoons fresh lime juice
1 tablespoon minced fresh ginger
1 tablespoon tomato paste
1 teaspoon cumin
1 teaspoon chili powder
¼ teaspoon salt
½ teaspoon Louisiana-style red hot pepper sauce
2 tablespoons water
¼ cup coarsely chopped cilantro or fresh basil
2 scallions, thinly sliced
1 can (19 ounces) black beans, rinsed and drained
1 cup coarsely chopped tomato

1 In a small saucepan of simmering water, cook the garlic for 3 minutes to blanch. Drain well.

2 In a food processor, combine the blanched garlic, lime juice, ginger, tomato paste, cumin, chili powder, salt, hot pepper sauce, and water, and process until blended.

3 Add the cilantro, scallions, and beans, and process with on/off pulses until combined but still chunky. Transfer the dip to a serving bowl and stir in the tomato. *Makes 2 cups*

Curried White Bean Dip Use a 19-ounce can of cannellini beans instead of the black beans, and curry powder instead of chili powder. Stir in 2 tablespoons of chopped mango chutney.

per serving	
calories	137
total fat	3.4g
saturated fat	0.3g
cholesterol	0mg
dietary fiber	1g
carbohydrate	24g
protein	4g
sodium	299mg

Spicy Italian Chips

If you can't find tomato-basil tortillas, substitute another flavored tortilla or even plain tortillas. Serve the chips on their own, with salsa, or with a chunky bean dip.

¼ cup fresh lemon juice
2 teaspoons olive oil
1 teaspoon garlic powder
½ teaspoon oregano
½ teaspoon cayenne pepper
¼ teaspoon salt
4 sun-dried tomato-basil flour tortillas (8 inches),
    each cut into 8 wedges

1 Preheat the oven to 400°F. Line 2 large baking sheets with foil and spray the foil with nonstick cooking spray.

2 In a small bowl, whisk together the lemon juice, olive oil, garlic powder, oregano, cayenne, and salt. Dip the tortillas wedges into the lemon mixture.

3 Place the tortilla wedges on the baking sheets and bake 8 to 10 minutes, or until crisp and lightly browned, turning them over halfway through the baking time.

4 Transfer the chips to a wire rack to cool. *Makes 4 servings*

Spicy Mexican Chips Use lime juice instead of lemon juice, and ground cumin in place of the oregano.

Portobello "Pizzas"

Big, meaty portobello mushrooms stand in for the crust in these "pizzas."

KITCHEN tip
Scraping the gills (the dark feathery undersides) off the portobello mushrooms keeps them from releasing as much liquid when they cook.

8 large portobello mushrooms (4 ounces each), stems removed and reserved
¼ cup water
3 cloves garlic, minced
¾ teaspoon salt
1 cup cooked white beans (rinsed and drained if canned)
1 cup cherry tomatoes, halved
1 cup arugula or watercress leaves, torn into bite-size pieces
4 tablespoons grated Parmesan cheese
2 teaspoons balsamic vinegar

1 Preheat the oven to 400°F. With a small spoon, scrape out and discard the black gills from the mushroom caps. Spray a jelly-roll pan with nonstick cooking spray. Place the mushroom caps, stemmed-side down, in the pan and cover them with foil.

2 Bake until the mushroom caps are tender, about 7 minutes. Transfer the baked mushroom caps, stemmed-side down, to paper towels to drain. Discard any liquid left in the jelly-roll pan. Leave the oven on.

3 Meanwhile, finely chop the mushroom stems. In a large nonstick skillet, heat the water over medium heat. Add the garlic and mushroom stems, and cook, stirring frequently, until the stems are tender and the liquid has been absorbed, about 5 minutes. Transfer to a large bowl and add ¼ teaspoon of the salt, the beans, cherry tomatoes, arugula, 1 tablespoon of the Parmesan, and the vinegar.

4 Return the baked mushroom caps to the jelly-roll pan, stemmed-side up. Sprinkle the mushrooms with the remaining ½ teaspoon salt. Fill the mushroom cavities with the bean mixture and sprinkle with the remaining 3 tablespoons Parmesan. Bake until the bean mixture is piping hot and the Parmesan is crusty, about 5 minutes. Serve hot or at room temperature. *Makes 8 "pizzas"*

Sesame-Ginger Tofu

Pass the toothpicks and serve these as you would cubes of cheese. The citrusy soy marinade gets absorbed halfway up the tofu for an interesting contrast in flavors.

per cube	
calories	18
total fat	1g
saturated fat	0.2g
cholesterol	0mg
dietary fiber	0g
carbohydrate	1g
protein	2g
sodium	55mg

ON THE Menu

Tofu is extremely healthful, but it is not low in fat (though the fat is mostly unsaturated). So, if you serve this as an appetizer, keep the fat low in the main course.

15 ounces extra-firm tofu
1/3 cup water
2 tablespoons minced fresh ginger
3 cloves garlic, minced
3 tablespoons reduced-sodium soy sauce
3 tablespoons fresh lime juice
2 teaspoons dark brown sugar
1 teaspoon dark sesame oil
2 scallions, thinly sliced

1 Slice the block of tofu horizontally. Place the two slabs of tofu on a paper towel-lined cutting board. Cover the tofu with more paper towels and place a heavy skillet on top of the paper towels. Put something under one end of the cutting board to tilt it at a slight angle and place the opposite end of the cutting board at the edge of the sink so the tofu can drain. Let stand 3 hours at room temperature.

2 Meanwhile, in a small saucepan, bring the water to a boil over medium heat. Add the ginger and garlic and cook until the garlic is tender, about 2 minutes. Transfer the ginger, garlic, and any liquid remaining in the saucepan to a large shallow nonreactive pan and stir in the soy sauce, lime juice, sugar, and sesame oil.

3 Cut each slab of drained tofu into 15 cubes and place in the pan with the soy mixture. Let stand for 2 hours or until the soy mixture has been absorbed halfway up the cubes of tofu (the top half of the tofu will remain white, while the bottom will be dark). Refrigerate and serve chilled.

4 At serving time, scatter the scallions over the tofu cubes. *Makes 30 cubes*

Spotlite recipe

Chinese Dumplings

Wonton wrappers (also called wonton skins) are very thin squares of egg-pasta dough used to make a variety of little dumplings, including the Chinese soup dumplings called wontons. Wonton wrappers come 40 to 50 wrappers per package. Although we've used them to make appetizers, these dumplings would also make a delicious light lunch or dinner served in a hot broth. To serve four people, bring 4 cups of homemade broth—Chicken, Roasted Vegetable, or Garlic Broth (*see page 32*)—to a boil. Add 12 dumplings and cook 2 minutes. Serve topped with a sprinkling of sliced scallions.

4 tablespoons reduced-sodium soy sauce
2 tablespoons minced fresh ginger
2 cloves garlic, minced
½ pound lean ground turkey
¼ cup minced cilantro
¼ cup minced fresh mint
24 wonton wrappers (3½ inches square)
¼ cup fresh lime juice
2 teaspoons sugar

1 In a medium bowl, combine 2 tablespoons of the soy sauce, the ginger, and garlic. Add the ground turkey, cilantro, and mint, and mix well.

2 Place the wonton wrappers on a work surface. Spoon a generous 2 teaspoons of the turkey mixture onto the center of each wrapper. Moisten the edges of a wrapper with a finger dipped in water. Fold one corner of the square over the filling onto the diagonally opposite corner to make a triangle. Press to seal.

3 In a large pot of boiling water, cook half the dumplings at a time until firm, about 2 minutes. Scoop out with a slotted spoon and drain briefly on a double layer of paper towels. Bring the water back to a boil and repeat with the remaining dumplings.

4 Meanwhile, in a small bowl, combine the remaining 2 tablespoons soy sauce, the lime juice, and sugar. Serve the dumplings with the soy-lime dipping sauce on the side. ***Makes 24 dumplings***

PER DUMPLING 41 calories, 0.8g total fat (0.2g saturated), 1mg cholesterol, 0g dietary fiber, 6g carbohydrate, 3g protein, 142mg sodium

Salmon & Dill Pita Pizzas

Instead of serving these as an appetizer, you could serve a whole pita pizza for a light lunch. If you can't find fresh dill, stir 1 teaspoon of dried dillweed into the yogurt.

4 whole-wheat pita breads (7 inches)
¼ cup tomato paste
2 cups cherry tomatoes, halved
1 large red onion, halved and thinly sliced
3 cloves garlic, minced
1 tablespoon olive oil
½ teaspoon salt
¾ cup flaked, canned pink salmon
½ cup plain fat-free yogurt
¼ cup minced fresh dill

1 Preheat the oven to 450°F. Brush one side of each pita with tomato paste and place the pitas on a large baking sheet.

2 In a medium bowl, toss together the cherry tomatoes, onion, garlic, oil, and salt. Scatter the tomato-onion mixture over the pitas. Bake 8 to 10 minutes, or until the pitas are crisp.

3 Scatter the salmon, yogurt, and dill on top of the tomato mixture and bake until the salmon is heated through, about 3 minutes. Cut each pita into 4 wedges. **Makes 16 wedges**

Tuna & Basil Pita Pizzas Use water-packed albacore tuna instead of salmon and minced fresh basil instead of dill.

per wedge	
calories	75
total fat	1.9g
saturated fat	0.3g
cholesterol	3mg
dietary fiber	2g
carbohydrate	12g
protein	4g
sodium	234mg

good source of:
selenium

KITCHEN tip

One of the best ways to "mince" the feathery fronds of fresh dill is with a pair of scissors. Just hold the dill sprigs over a bowl and use the scissors to snip the herb into tiny pieces.

Caramelized Onion & Apple Focaccia

This rendition of the classic Italian flatbread is served here as an hors d'oeuvre, but you can also serve it as a bread to go along with a meal. Cut it into larger portions and serve with a soup or salad.

1 package (¼ ounce) active dry yeast
1 teaspoon sugar
1½ cups warm (105°F to 115°F) water
2½ cups all-purpose flour
1 cup whole-wheat flour
½ cup grated Parmesan cheese
2½ teaspoons salt
½ teaspoon cayenne pepper
¼ cup olive oil
3 pounds Spanish onions, cut in eighths and thickly sliced
1 pound apples, quartered and thinly sliced

1 In a large bowl, sprinkle the yeast and sugar over ½ cup of the warm water. Let stand 5 minutes or until foamy. Stir in the all-purpose flour, whole-wheat flour, 6 tablespoons of the Parmesan, 1½ teaspoons of the salt, and the cayenne until blended. Stir in 3 tablespoons of the oil and the remaining 1 cup warm water until well combined. Transfer to a lightly floured work surface and knead until smooth and elastic.

2 Transfer to a lightly oiled large bowl, turning the dough to coat. Cover and let stand 1 hour in a warm draft-free spot until doubled.

3 Meanwhile, in a large nonstick Dutch oven or flameproof casserole, heat the remaining 1 tablespoon oil over low heat. Add the onions and remaining 1 teaspoon salt and cook, stirring often, for 1 hour, or until the onions are very soft and golden brown. Set aside to cool to room temperature.

4 Punch the dough down, transfer to a lightly oiled jelly-roll pan or large baking sheet, and pat the dough out to a 15 x 11-inch rectangle. Cover and let stand 45 minutes, or until puffed and well risen.

5 Preheat the oven to 425°F. Sprinkle the apples, caramelized onions, and remaining 2 tablespoons Parmesan over the dough. Cover and let rise 30 minutes. Uncover and bake on the lowest level of the oven for 25 minutes, or until the crust is golden brown and crisp. Cut into 20 rectangles. *Makes 20 pieces*

per piece	
calories	152
total fat	4g
saturated fat	0.9g
cholesterol	2mg
dietary fiber	3g
carbohydrate	26g
protein	4g
sodium	340mg

good source of:
selenium, thiamin

F.Y.I.

Onions are notable not only for their contribution to cooking, but also for their potential to protect against disease. Along with their savory, pungent flavor, onions supply fiber, vitamin C, potassium and vitamin B_6. Some evidence shows that natural plant chemicals (phytochemicals) in onions called flavonoids may protect against oxidative damage to cells by mopping up harmful free-radical molecules.

ON THE *Menu*

This chunky soup could be a meal in itself. Serve it with a salad of shredded hearts of romaine tossed with a fat-free lemon vinaigrette.

Chunky Potato, Mushroom & Broccoli Soup

Broccoli, potatoes, and smoky dried mushrooms give this soup a wonderful earthy flavor. If you use dried shiitake mushrooms, remove and discard the inedible stems either before or after soaking.

½ cup dried porcini or shiitake mushrooms (½ ounce)
2 cups warm water
1 tablespoon olive oil
1 large red onion, finely chopped
4 cloves garlic, minced
1 pound red potatoes, cut into small chunks
1 teaspoon salt
¾ teaspoon tarragon
2½ cups small broccoli florets
½ cup fat-free half-and-half

1 In a small bowl, combine the dried mushrooms and 1 cup of warm water and let stand for 20 minutes until softened. Reserving the soaking liquid, scoop out the dried mushrooms and coarsely chop. Strain the soaking liquid through a coffee filter or a paper towel-lined sieve.

2 Meanwhile, in a large nonstick saucepan, heat the oil over medium heat. Add the onion and garlic, and cook, stirring frequently, until the onion is golden brown, about 5 minutes.

3 Stir in the mushrooms and their soaking liquid, the potatoes, salt, tarragon, and remaining 1 cup water, and bring to a boil. Reduce to a simmer, cover, and cook for 10 minutes.

4 Add the broccoli and cook until the potatoes and broccoli are tender, about 5 minutes. Stir in the half-and-half and cook just until heated through, about 2 minutes. *Makes 4 servings*

Greek Orzo-Vegetable Soup

For a heartier soup, stir cooked shrimp, shredded cooked chicken, or crumbled feta cheese into the soup just before serving. Serve with wedges of toasted pita bread.

per serving	
calories	181
total fat	3g
saturated fat	0.4g
cholesterol	0mg
dietary fiber	4g
carbohydrate	31g
protein	8g
sodium	685mg

good source of: beta carotene, folate, niacin, riboflavin, selenium, thiamin, vitamin C

2 teaspoons olive oil
4 scallions, thinly sliced
3 cloves garlic, minced
2 carrots, halved lengthwise and thinly sliced
3 cups chicken broth, homemade (*page 32*) or
    reduced-sodium canned
1 cup water
½ teaspoon salt
½ cup orzo
¾ cup minced fresh dill
1 cup frozen peas
2 tablespoons fresh lemon juice
1 teaspoon cornstarch blended with 1 tablespoon water

F.Y.I.

Orzo is a small pasta shape that resembles large grains of rice or unhulled barley (the Italian word *orzo* means barley). It's often used as a "soup pasta," which means tiny pasta shapes that cook up quickly in soups. Orzo can also be served as a pasta dish, tossed with a sauce, or served as a simple side dish like rice.

1 In a large nonstick saucepan, heat the oil over low heat. Add the scallions and garlic, and cook, stirring frequently, until the scallions are tender, about 3 minutes.

2 Stir in the carrots and cook 3 minutes. Add the broth, water, and salt, and bring to a boil. Add the orzo and ½ cup of the dill. Cover and cook until the orzo is tender, about 8 minutes.

3 Stir in the remaining ¼ cup dill, the peas, and lemon juice, and cook until the peas are heated through, about 2 minutes. Stir in the cornstarch mixture and cook, stirring, until the soup is slightly thickened, about 1 minute.
Makes 4 servings

Vegetarian Orzo Soup Substitute 3 cups of Roasted Vegetable Broth or Garlic Broth (*both on page 32*) for the chicken broth.

"Cream" of Tomato-Basil Soup

The "cream" is actually silken tofu—Japanese-style tofu, which is softer and smoother in texture than regular tofu, and a surprisingly successful substitute for heavy cream in this soup recipe.

2 large onions, finely chopped
12 large cloves garlic, minced
3¼ cups water
2 yellow bell peppers, diced
1 can (28 ounces) crushed tomatoes
1 can (29 ounces) no-salt-added tomato puree
2 teaspoons grated orange zest
1 cup orange juice
4 cups broccoli florets
½ cup chopped fresh basil
1 package (19 ounces) soft silken tofu, drained

1   In a nonstick Dutch oven or flameproof casserole, combine the onion, garlic, and ¾ cup of the water, and cook, stirring frequently, over low heat until the onion is tender, about 7 minutes. Add the bell peppers and cook, stirring frequently, until the peppers are tender, about 5 minutes.

2   Stir in the crushed tomatoes, tomato puree, orange zest, orange juice, and remaining 2½ cups water, and bring to a boil. Reduce to a simmer and cook for 7 minutes to blend the flavors.

3   Add the broccoli and basil to the simmering soup and cook until the broccoli is cooked through, about 7 minutes.

4   In a food processor, puree the tofu until very smooth and creamy. Add ½ cup of the tomato liquid from the soup to the food processor and puree until well combined. Stir the pureed tofu mixture into the soup and cook gently just until heated through. ***Makes 6 servings***

per serving	
calories	241
total fat	5.9g
saturated fat	0.8g
cholesterol	0mg
dietary fiber	11g
carbohydrate	41g
protein	13g
sodium	450mg

good source of: beta carotene, calcium, fiber, folate, magnesium, niacin, potassium, riboflavin, thiamin, vitamin B_6, vitamin C, vitamin E, zinc

ON THE *Menu*

You can have this soup as a light lunch or a first course, or you can make it into a main course by adding a batch of turkey meatballs (*see page 70*). Add them to the simmering soup in step 3 and cook for about 7 minutes, or until the meatballs are cooked through.

Cream of Sweet Potato-Apple Soup

Serve this simple-to-make soup as a main course, with a loaf of warm, crusty peasant bread and a vinaigrette-dressed green salad.

per serving	
calories	123
total fat	0.4g
saturated fat	0.1g
cholesterol	1mg
dietary fiber	3g
carbohydrate	28g
protein	3g
sodium	587mg

good source of: beta carotene, fiber, potassium, riboflavin, vitamin B$_6$, vitamin C, vitamin E

F.Y.I.

The sweet potato provides most of the vitamin B$_6$ in this soup. Smaller amounts come from the onions, milk and apple juice. Vitamin B$_6$, along with folate, may protect against heart disease by lowering levels of homocysteine. High blood levels of homocysteine increase the odds for heart disease. Vitamin B$_6$ is essential for the manufacture of substances known as prostaglandins, which are involved in processes such as blood pressure regulation and heart function. And vitamin B$_6$ is also necessary for red blood cell formation.

1½ teaspoons cumin
2 cups water
2 tablespoons frozen apple juice concentrate
¾ pound sweet potatoes, peeled and cut into chunks
1 large Granny Smith apple, peeled and cut into chunks
1 medium onion, cut into chunks
¾ teaspoon salt
½ teaspoon pepper
½ cup fat-free milk
2 tablespoons plain fat-free yogurt (optional)
1 tablespoon chopped cilantro or parsley

1 In a Dutch oven or flameproof casserole, toast the cumin over medium heat, shaking and stirring the pan frequently, until fragrant and toasted, about 3 minutes.

2 Add the water, apple juice concentrate, sweet potatoes, apple, onion, salt, and pepper. Cover and bring to a boil over high heat. Reduce the heat to medium-low and simmer until the sweet potatoes and apple are tender, about 20 minutes.

3 Transfer the soup to a food processor or blender and puree. Return the puree to the pan and add the milk. Cook over medium heat, stirring frequently, until heated through.

4 Ladle the soup into bowls, top with yogurt (if using), and sprinkle with the cilantro. ***Makes 4 servings***

Garlicky Sweet Potato & Apple Soup Substitute 2 cups of Garlic Broth (*page 32*) for the water.

Curried Red Lentil-Carrot Soup

Mildly sweet carrot juice brings out the flavors of the spices in this curried soup. Look for red lentils in Indian grocery stores.

2 teaspoons olive oil
1 large onion, coarsely chopped
2 cloves garlic, minced
2½ teaspoons curry powder
½ teaspoon salt
¼ teaspoon black pepper
⅛ teaspoon cayenne pepper
1 cup carrot juice
½ pound unpeeled all-purpose potatoes, cut into ½-inch
    chunks
1 cup red lentils, rinsed and picked over
2 medium carrots, sliced
1 bay leaf
3¼ cups water

1 In a large nonstick saucepan, heat the oil over medium-high heat. Add the onion and garlic, and cook until the onion is tender, 5 to 6 minutes. Stir in the curry powder, salt, black pepper, and cayenne pepper, and cook, stirring, for 30 seconds.

2 Add the carrot juice, potatoes, lentils, carrots, bay leaf, and water. Cover and bring to a boil over high heat. Reduce the heat to medium-low and simmer, stirring occasionally, until the lentils are tender, about 20 minutes. Remove and discard the bay leaf before serving. ***Makes 6 servings***

Potato Soup with Chicken & Green Chilies

per serving	
calories	305
total fat	5.4g
saturated fat	1g
cholesterol	34mg
dietary fiber	6g
carbohydrate	39g
protein	18g
sodium	575mg

good source of: niacin, potassium, selenium, vitamin B_6, vitamin C

For an even more substantial soup with an extra flourish of Tex-Mex flavor, add 1 cup of frozen corn kernels when you're adding the chicken, and top the soup with diced avocado and a dollop of sour cream.

> 1 tablespoon olive oil
> 1 red bell pepper, cut into ½-inch squares
> 4 scallions, sliced
> 3 cloves garlic, minced
> 1½ pounds all-purpose potatoes, peeled and cut into ½-inch cubes
> 3 cups water
> 3 tablespoons flour
> 1 cup chicken broth, homemade (*page 32*) or reduced-sodium canned
> ¾ cup dry white wine
> 1 tablespoon plus 1 teaspoon chili powder
> 1 teaspoon ground coriander
> ½ teaspoon salt
> 1 can (4 ounces) chopped mild green chilies, drained
> ½ pound skinless, boneless chicken breast, cut into ½-inch chunks
> 3 tablespoons chopped cilantro

KITCHEN tip

Here's a trick if you don't have canned green chilies on hand. Dice a green bell pepper and microwave it, loosely covered, with a squeeze of lemon juice and a dash of hot pepper sauce. Cook just until the pepper is softened. Start out with 45 seconds on high power and then check it; continue in small increments of time until the diced pepper is soft.

1 In a large saucepan, heat the oil over medium heat. Add the bell pepper, scallions, garlic, and potatoes. Cover and cook, stirring frequently, until the pepper is tender, about 7 minutes.

2 Meanwhile, in a small bowl, stir the water into the flour until blended.

3 Add the broth, wine, chili powder, coriander, salt, and green chilies to the saucepan. Bring to a simmer, stir in the flour mixture, and cook until the potatoes are firm-tender, about 10 minutes.

4 Add the chicken and cook until the chicken is cooked through, 2 to 3 minutes. Stir in the cilantro and serve. ***Makes 4 servings***

Winter Squash & Lemon Soup

This autumnal soup is sweet and creamy without any cream. A nice accompaniment would be very thin slices of toasted sourdough bread and a tossed escarole salad with a simple vinaigrette.

per serving	
calories	118
total fat	2.6g
saturated fat	0.4g
cholesterol	0mg
dietary fiber	2g
carbohydrate	24g
protein	3g
sodium	306mg

good source of: beta carotene, vitamin C

2 teaspoons olive oil
1 medium onion, finely chopped
1 clove garlic, minced
1½ teaspoons cumin
¼ teaspoon cayenne pepper
¼ teaspoon nutmeg
1 package (12 ounces) frozen winter squash puree, thawed
1½ cups water
2 tablespoons light brown sugar
½ teaspoon salt
1 tablespoon fresh lemon juice
¼ cup plain fat-free yogurt

1 In a medium nonstick saucepan, heat the oil over medium heat. Add the onion and garlic, and cook, stirring frequently, until the onion is tender, about 5 minutes.

2 Add the cumin, cayenne, and nutmeg, stirring to combine. Stir in the winter squash, water, brown sugar, and salt, and bring to a boil. Reduce to a simmer, cover, and cook 10 minutes to blend the flavors.

3 Remove from the heat and stir in the lemon juice. Serve hot, topped with a dollop of yogurt. ***Makes 4 servings***

Pumpkin Lime Soup Use 1½ cups canned unsweetened pumpkin puree instead of the winter squash puree. Substitute fresh lime juice for the lemon juice. Omit the cumin, cayenne, and nutmeg, and use 2 teaspoons chili powder instead.

F.Y.I.

The more orange the flesh of a winter squash, the more beta carotene it has. For example, yellow-fleshed acorn squash has only 0.5 gram of beta carotene per cup, while deep-orange butternut squash has 17 times as much (8.5 grams per cup).

broths

Chicken Broth

6 pounds whole chicken legs

8½ cups water

4 cups carrot juice

1 cup low-sodium tomato-
  vegetable juice

2 large onions, unpeeled, halved

2 large carrots, thickly sliced

1 large leek, thinly sliced

2 stalks celery, thinly sliced

8 cloves garlic, unpeeled

¾ teaspoon rosemary

¾ teaspoon thyme

10 sprigs of parsley

2 bay leaves

1 Preheat the oven to 450°F. Spread the chicken in a roasting pan and roast until browned and crisp, about 30 minutes.

2 Transfer the chicken to a large stockpot. Pour off all the fat from the roasting pan and add ½ cup of water to the pan, scraping up any browned bits. Add these juices to the stockpot with the chicken.

3 Add the remaining 8 cups water, carrot juice and tomato-vegetable juice, and bring to a boil over high heat, skimming off any foam as it rises to the surface. Continue skimming until no foam remains.

4 Add the onions, carrots, leek, celery, garlic, rosemary, thyme, parsley, and bay leaves. Return to a boil, continuing to skim any foam that rises. Reduce the heat to low and simmer until the broth is rich and flavorful, about 2 hours.

5 Strain and discard the solids. Refrigerate and remove the fat that solidifies on the surface. Refrigerate for up to 3 days or freeze for longer storage. **Makes about 7 cups**

PER ½ CUP: 56 CALORIES, 2.5G TOTAL FAT (0.6G SATURATED), 3MG CHOLESTEROL, 1G DIETARY FIBER, 7G CARBOHYDRATE, 1G PROTEIN, 46MG SODIUM. **GOOD SOURCE OF:** BETA CAROTENE

Roasted Vegetable Broth

4 large carrots, thickly sliced

2 large onions, unpeeled and
  quartered

3 stalks celery, cut in thirds

8 ounces mushrooms, halved

1 large tomato (8 ounces), cut
  into large chunks

6 cloves garlic, unpeeled

8½ cups water

1 bay leaf

8 sprigs of parsley

½ teaspoon tarragon

½ teaspoon salt

1 Preheat the oven to 450°F. Place the carrots, onions, celery, mushrooms, tomato, and garlic in a 9 x 13-inch roasting pan. Add ½ cup water and bake, shaking the pan occasionally, until the water has evaporated and the vegetables are richly browned, about 30 minutes.

2 Transfer the vegetables to a Dutch oven or large saucepan. Pour 2 cups of water into the roasting pan and scrape up any browned bits from the the pan. Pour this and the remaining 6 cups of water into the Dutch oven. Add the bay leaf, parsley, tarragon, and salt.

3 Bring the broth to a boil over high heat. Reduce to a simmer, partially cover, and cook until the broth is richly flavored, about 1¼ hours. Strain the broth and discard the solids. **Makes about 5 cups**

PER ½ CUP: 40 CALORIES, 0.2G TOTAL FAT (0G SATURATED), 0MG CHOLESTEROL, 0G DIETARY FIBER, 9G CARBOHYDRATE, 2G PROTEIN, 141MG SODIUM. **GOOD SOURCE OF:** BETA CAROTENE, POTASSIUM

Garlic Broth

5 large heads of garlic (1 pound),
  separated into cloves but
  unpeeled

2 stalks celery, thickly sliced

3 strips of lemon zest

½ teaspoon rosemary

½ teaspoon thyme

¼ teaspoon salt

8 cups water

Lightly smash about half the garlic cloves (leaving the skin on). In a large saucepan, combine the garlic, celery, lemon zest, rosemary, thyme, salt, and water. Bring to a boil over high heat. Reduce to a simmer, partially cover, and cook until the broth is full-flavored, about 1 hour. Strain and discard solids. **Makes about 5 cups**

PER ½ CUP: 47 CALORIES, 0.2G TOTAL FAT (0G SATURATED), 0MG CHOLESTEROL, 0G DIETARY FIBER, 11G CARBOHYDRATE, 2G PROTEIN, 70MG SODIUM. **GOOD SOURCE OF:** VITAMIN B_6

Chicken & Corn Tortilla Soup

If you prefer, substitute storebought baked corn tortilla chips for the fresh tortillas and omit step 1 of the recipe.

per serving	
calories	301
total fat	7.7g
saturated fat	1g
cholesterol	49mg
dietary fiber	3g
carbohydrate	34g
protein	25g
sodium	598mg

good source of: niacin, selenium, vitamin B_6

2 teaspoons olive oil
3 corn tortillas (6 inches), cut into ½-inch-wide strips
4 scallions, thinly sliced
3 cloves garlic, minced
1 large tomato, coarsely chopped
3 cups chicken broth, homemade (*page 32*) or reduced-sodium canned
1 teaspoon cumin
½ teaspoon oregano
¼ teaspoon salt
12 ounces skinless, boneless chicken breasts, cut crosswise into ¼-inch-wide strips
1 cup frozen corn kernels
2 tablespoons fresh lime juice

1 In a nonstick Dutch oven or flameproof casserole, heat the oil over medium heat. Add the tortilla strips and cook until lightly crisped, about 1 minute. With a slotted spoon, transfer the strips to paper towels to drain.

2 Add the scallions and garlic to the pan and cook until the scallions are tender, about 1 minute. Stir in the tomato, broth, cumin, oregano, and salt, and bring to a boil. Reduce to a simmer, cover, and cook until the flavors have developed, about 5 minutes.

3 Add the chicken strips and corn. Cover and cook until the chicken is just cooked through, about 3 minutes. Stir in the tortilla strips and lime juice just before serving. ***Makes 4 servings***

Black Bean & Corn Tortilla Soup Substitute 3 cups of Roasted Vegetable Broth (opposite page) for the chicken broth. Omit the chicken and add 1 can (15 ounces) rinsed and drained black beans. Add the beans in step 3, when you add the corn.

Manhattan-Style Fresh Salmon Chowder

Somewhere between a soup and a stew, this chowder is hearty enough to be a meal. For a change, substitute chunks of cod or grouper, or sea scallops, for the salmon.

2 cups water
2 strips of turkey bacon, thinly sliced crosswise
1 small red onion, finely chopped
3 cloves garlic, minced
1 green bell pepper, diced
1 pound red potatoes, cut into ½-inch chunks
1 cup bottled clam juice, canned chicken broth, or
    homemade Garlic Broth (*page 32*)
½ teaspoon salt
1 can (14½ ounces) stewed tomatoes
2 tablespoons tomato paste
½ pound skinless salmon fillet, cut into ½-inch chunks
1½ cups frozen corn kernels

1 In a medium nonstick saucepan, bring ⅓ cup of the water to a boil over medium heat. Add the bacon, onion, garlic, and bell pepper, and cook, stirring frequently, until the onion is tender, about 10 minutes.

2 Stir in the potatoes, clam juice, salt, and remaining 1⅔ cups of water. Bring to a gentle boil and cook until the potatoes are firm-tender, about 7 minutes.

3 Stir in the tomatoes and tomato paste. Return to a boil. Add the salmon and corn. Reduce to a simmer, cover, and cook until the salmon is just cooked through, about 5 minutes. ***Makes 4 servings***

KITCHEN *tip*

Many soup recipes start out with aromatic vegetables (usually garlic and onion, and sometimes bell pepper) being cooked in oil. This helps to flavor the broth that will be the basis of the soup. However, there's no reason why the aromatics can't be cooked in water if you're looking to trim fat. Just bring a small amount of water to a boil in a nonstick skillet, then add the cut-up vegetables. Cook at a simmer until the liquid has evaporated and the vegetables are tender.

Gingered Carrot Soup

Next time you make a pot of brown rice, double the recipe and use some of the leftover rice in this sweet and spicy carrot soup.

2½ cups sliced carrots
1 large leek, sliced (about 2 cups)
2 cloves garlic, peeled
2 tablespoons chopped fresh ginger
1½ cups carrot juice
½ cup water
½ teaspoon salt
¼ teaspoon pepper
½ cup low-fat (1%) milk
1 cup cooked brown rice
2 tablespoons minced fresh mint or basil

1   In a large saucepan, combine the carrots, leek, garlic, ginger, carrot juice, water, salt, and pepper. Bring to a boil over high heat. Reduce to a simmer, cover, and cook until the vegetables are very tender, about 10 minutes.

2   Transfer to a food processor or blender. Add the milk and ½ cup of the cooked brown rice and puree until smooth.

3   Divide the remaining rice among 4 soup bowls. Ladle the hot soup on top and sprinkle with the mint. ***Makes 4 servings***

Carrot-Barley Soup Substitute cooked barley for the brown rice.

F.Y.I.

A heart-healthy whole grain, brown rice has had only the outer hull removed, which means that it retains nutrients such as thiamin, niacin, and vitamin B₆ that are lost when the germ and bran layers are stripped in processing white rice. And, because it still has its fiber-rich bran layer, brown rice is also an excellent source of fiber. In fact, 1 cup of brown rice supplies more than five times as much fiber as 1 cup of white rice.

Creamy Basil-Pea Soup

While romaine might seem an odd soup ingredient, the lettuce lightens the texture of the soup once it's been pureed.

per serving	
calories	171
total fat	4.1g
saturated fat	1.2g
cholesterol	4mg
dietary fiber	9g
carbohydrate	24g
protein	11g
sodium	666mg

good source of: fiber, folate, potassium, thiamin

2 teaspoons olive oil
6 scallions, thinly sliced
3 cloves garlic, minced
¾ cup split peas
1 cup shredded romaine lettuce
½ cup packed basil leaves
1 teaspoon salt
½ teaspoon pepper
½ teaspoon oregano
4½ cups water
⅔ cup low-fat (1%) milk
¼ cup grated Parmesan cheese

1 In a large nonstick saucepan, heat the oil over medium heat. Add the scallions and garlic, and cook until the scallions are tender, about 2 minutes.

2 Stir in the split peas, lettuce, basil, salt, pepper, oregano, and water, and bring to a boil. Reduce to a simmer, cover, and cook until the split peas are tender, about 45 minutes.

3 Working in batches, transfer the soup to a food processor and puree. Return the puree to the pan, add the milk, and gently heat over low heat.

4 Serve the soup sprinkled with Parmesan. *Makes 6 servings*

Creamy Basil-Lentil Soup Use lentils instead of split peas and substitute ground cumin for the oregano. Substitute Garlic Broth (*page 32*) for the water.

F.Y.I.

While many types of lettuce are nutritional lightweights, romaine is uncharacteristically rich in nutrients. Romaine provides an impressive collection of vitamins and minerals such as folate, potassium, and vitamin C. And the deep color of its leaves is a clue to the fact that romaine also contains a rich supply of the carotenoid beta carotene.

KITCHEN *tip*

If the sun-dried tomatoes you get are very soft, you can use them as is, but for many recipes, the tomatoes must be soaked in hot water to soften them before using (and sometimes the recipe also uses the tomato soaking water for added flavor).

Peppered Tuna with Plum Tomato & Cannellini Salad

Although this tuna is broiled, tuna steaks are a natural for an outdoor grill. You can make the cannellini salad well ahead of time and bring it outside when you're ready to grill the fish.

¼ cup sun-dried tomatoes (not oil-packed)
½ cup boiling water
2 cups canned cannellini or other white beans, rinsed and drained
2 plum tomatoes, seeded and diced
½ cup diced red onion
¼ cup diced red bell pepper
¼ cup chopped flat-leaf parsley
3 tablespoons red wine vinegar
1 tablespoon plus 1 teaspoon extra-virgin olive oil
2 teaspoons coarsely cracked black pepper
½ teaspoon salt
4 tuna steaks (5 ounces each)

1 In a small heatproof bowl, combine the sun-dried tomatoes and boiling water. Let stand until the tomatoes have softened, 15 to 20 minutes (depending on the dryness of the tomatoes). Drain and coarsely chop.

2 In a large bowl, combine the chopped sun-dried tomatoes, beans, plum tomatoes, onion, bell pepper, parsley, vinegar, 1 tablespoon of the olive oil, ½ teaspoon of the black pepper, and ¼ teaspoon of the salt. Mix well and set aside at room temperature to blend the flavors.

3 Preheat the broiler. Spray a broiler pan with nonstick cooking spray.

4 Rub the tuna with the remaining 1 teaspoon olive oil. Sprinkle with the remaining 1½ teaspoons pepper and ¼ teaspoon salt. Broil the tuna 4 to 6 inches from the heat, turning it over once, for 8 minutes, or until just slightly pink in center.

5 Divide the beans among 4 plates and place the grilled tuna steak on top. *Makes 4 servings*

Orange-Ginger Salmon

This marinade would work equally well with another fish steak or on chicken or pork.

4 salmon steaks (6 ounces each)
¼ cup orange marmalade
2 tablespoons reduced-sodium soy sauce
2 tablespoons balsamic vinegar
1 tablespoon grated fresh ginger
1 tablespoon dark sesame oil
1 clove garlic, minced
¼ teaspoon salt
¼ teaspoon pepper

1 In a shallow glass or ceramic dish large enough to hold the salmon in a single layer, combine the marmalade, soy sauce, vinegar, ginger, sesame oil, garlic, salt, and pepper.

2 Add the salmon, turning to coat. Cover and marinate in the refrigerator for at least 30 minutes and up to 2 hours.

3 Preheat the broiler. Lift the salmon from the marinade, transfer to a broiler pan, and spoon the marinade over the fish. Broil 4 to 6 inches from the heat for 3 to 4 minutes per side, or until the salmon just flakes when tested with a fork. Remove the salmon skin before eating. ***Makes 4 servings***

Pineapple-Ginger Salmon Make the Pineapple-Ginger Marinade (*page 56*) instead of this marinade. Skip step 1 and then follow the marinating and cooking directions in steps 2 and 3.

ON THE *Menu*
Serve this delicious salmon dish with cooked barley, steamed asparagus, and a salad of chopped watercress with a fat-free balsamic vinaigrette.

Shrimp Stir-Fry with Shiitake & Asparagus

Though cleaned shrimp are more costly, they are a distinct timesaver. Shelling and deveining shrimp for a stir-fry can take more time than actually cooking the dish.

per serving	
calories	176
total fat	6g
saturated fat	0.9g
cholesterol	119mg
dietary fiber	2g
carbohydrate	10g
protein	19g
sodium	681mg

good source of: selenium, vitamin B$_{12}$, vitamin D

3 tablespoons reduced-sodium soy sauce
3 tablespoons fresh lemon juice
1 teaspoon dark sesame oil
1 teaspoon cornstarch
¾ pound medium shrimp, shelled and deveined
1 tablespoon olive oil
4 scallions, cut into 1-inch lengths
2 cloves garlic, finely chopped
1 tablespoon minced fresh ginger
½ pound asparagus, cut on the diagonal into 1-inch lengths
½ pound shiitake mushrooms, stems discarded and caps quartered
¼ teaspoon salt

1 In a medium bowl, combine the soy sauce, lemon juice, sesame oil, and cornstarch. Add the shrimp, tossing to coat. Cover and refrigerate for 30 minutes.

2 In a large nonstick skillet, heat the olive oil over medium heat. Add the scallions, garlic, and ginger, and stir-fry until softened, about 1 minute. Add the asparagus, mushrooms, and salt, and stir-fry until the asparagus are crisp-tender, about 4 minutes.

3 Reserving the marinade, add the shrimp to the pan and stir-fry until the shrimp are beginning to turn pink but are not opaque, about 3 minutes. Add the reserved marinade and cook, stirring, until the shrimp are opaque throughout and the sauce is slightly thickened, about 1 minute. ***Makes 4 servings***

Chicken Stir-Fry with Shiitake & Asparagus If you don't care for shrimp, you can make this stir-fry with chicken instead. Use ¾ pound of skinless, boneless chicken breast cut crosswise into ½-inch-wide strips. Add it to the pan in step 3, when you would have added the shrimp. Cook for 4 minutes, then add the marinade and continue cooking as directed.

Spotlite recipe

Parmesan Fish Sticks

Making your own fish
sticks may seem like an
odd idea (given the prolif-
eration of commercial
brands), but if you try this
extremely easy recipe, you
will never look back: An
equivalent serving of commercial fish sticks has 100
more calories and almost
four times the fat and saturated fat. We've chosen
tilapia, which is a sturdy
and meaty (but mild-tast-
ing) fish; but you could
also use grouper or snap-
per. Serve the fish sticks as
is, with a squeeze of fresh
lemon, or with one of our
homemade dipping sauces
(*page 43*). While any of
these dipping sauces
would go nicely with the
fish sticks, the Balsamic-
Ketchup Sauce works par-
ticularly well.

1 pound skinless tilapia fillets
¼ cup flour
2 large egg whites beaten with 1 tablespoon water
¼ cup plain dried breadcrumbs
¼ cup grated Parmesan cheese
¼ teaspoon salt

1 Preheat the oven to 450°F. Spray a large baking sheet with nonstick
cooking spray. Cut the fillets into 1 x 2-inch strips. Dip the fish first in the
flour, then in the egg white mixture.

2 In a shallow bowl, combine the breadcrumbs, Parmesan, and salt. Dip
the fish strips in the breadcrumb mixture, patting the mixture into the
fish. Place on the baking sheet.

3 Bake, turning the fish over midway, for 10 minutes, or until the fish is
crusty, golden brown, and cooked through. ***Makes 4 servings***

PER SERVING 205 calories, 3.8g total fat (1.6g saturated), 47mg cholesterol, 0g
dietary fiber, 11g carbohydrate, 29g protein, 420mg sodium
Good source of: selenium, vitamin B$_{12}$

Tandoori Salmon

An Indian tandoor (clay oven) gets extremely hot, which is why the oven temperature is set to 500°F for this baked fish. Roast the salmon in the middle of the oven to get the most even heat distribution.

1 teaspoon cumin
⅓ cup plain low-fat yogurt
1 clove garlic
1 tablespoon peeled, thinly sliced fresh ginger
1½ teaspoons paprika
½ teaspoon salt
¼ teaspoon cardamom
⅛ teaspoon cayenne pepper
2 large salmon steaks (10 ounces each), halved crosswise
Lemon wedges, for serving

1 In a small, ungreased skillet, toast the cumin over medium-low heat until fragrant and slightly darker in color, about 2 minutes. Transfer to a blender and add the yogurt, garlic, ginger, paprika, salt, cardamom, and cayenne, and puree until smooth.

2 With a small, sharp paring knife, make several shallow slashes in the salmon flesh. Place the salmon in a nonaluminum baking pan large enough to hold the fish in a single layer. Pour the yogurt marinade over the fish. Cover and refrigerate at least 4 hours (or up to overnight), turning the salmon over once.

3 Preheat the oven to 500°F. Remove the pan from the refrigerator and bring to room temperature. Bake the salmon for 10 minutes, or until it just flakes when tested with a fork. Serve with lemon wedges. ***Makes 4 servings***

ON THE *Menu*

Serve the salmon with aromatic rice (such as basmati or jasmine), mango chutney, and steamed green beans. For dessert, have fresh pineapple slices sprinkled with brown sugar.

Herb-Grilled Shrimp

You could serve the shrimp as is, or with one of the dipping sauces on the opposite page.

> 1½ teaspoons paprika
> ¾ teaspoon thyme
> ½ teaspoon salt
> ½ teaspoon pepper
> 1 pound large shrimp (about 24), shelled and deveined
> 2 teaspoons olive oil

1 Preheat the broiler. In a large bowl, combine the paprika, thyme, salt, and pepper. Add the shrimp and oil, and toss to coat.

2 Spray a broiler pan with nonstick cooking spray. Place the shrimp on the pan and broil 4 to 6 inches from the heat, turning once, for 2 to 3 minutes, or until the shrimp are opaque throughout. *Makes 4 servings*

Rosemary Shrimp Pasta Sauce Substitute minced rosemary for the thyme and reduce the amount to ½ teaspoon. After the shrimp are grilled and are cool enough to handle, cut them in half crosswise. Stir them into about 2 cups homemade or storebought marinara sauce. Cook 12 ounces of a pasta shape, such as shells or rotini, and toss with the marinara-shrimp sauce.

per serving	
calories	92
total fat	3.1g
saturated fat	0.5g
cholesterol	135mg
dietary fiber	0g
carbohydrate	1g
protein	15g
sodium	446mg

good source of: selenium, vitamin B_{12}, vitamin D

ON THE *Menu*

For a well-rounded meal, serve these shrimp (and a dipping sauce, if desired) with steamed broccoli and boiled new potatoes. For dessert, offer Wine-Poached Plums with Yogurt Cream (*page 135*).

HOMEMADE
dipping sauces

Here are some recipes from this book that would go nicely with any of these homemade dipping sauces:

- Chinese Dumplings (*page 22*): Use one of these dipping sauces in place of the sauce that's in the dumpling recipe.
- Parmesan Fish Sticks (*page 40*)
- Herb-Grilled Shrimp (*page 42*)
- Homemade meatballs (*page 70*): Serve the meatballs as appetizers with one or all of these dipping sauces.

Or, instead of using the sauce for dipping, use it as a condiment for any plain piece of broiled poultry or fish, or with any type of burger. Try one of these recipes:

- Salmon-Potato Loaf (*page 47*)
- Broiled Tuna or Salmon Burgers (*page 50*)
- Orange-Broiled Snapper (*page 52*)
- Extra-Moist Turkey Loaf (*page 79*)
- Shiitake Mushroom Burgers (*page 83*)

Balsamic-Ketchup Dipping Sauce

5 tablespoons ketchup
5 teaspoons balsamic vinegar
5 teaspoons honey

In a small bowl, stir together the ketchup, vinegar, and honey. **Makes ½ cup**

PER 2 TABLESPOONS: 51 CALORIES, 0.1G TOTAL FAT (0G SATURATED), 0MG CHOLESTEROL, 0G DIETARY FIBER, 13G CARBOHYDRATE, 0.3G PROTEIN, 229MG SODIUM

Lemon-Herb Dipping Sauce

1½ teaspoons ground cumin
1 cup plain fat-free yogurt
3 tablespoons chopped fresh mint
1 tablespoon minced chives or scallion greens
1 teaspoon grated lemon zest
1 tablespoon fresh lemon juice
½ teaspoon salt
¼ teaspoon pepper

1 In a small, ungreased skillet, toast the cumin over medium-low heat until fragrant and slightly darker in color, about 2 minutes. Immediately transfer to a small bowl so it won't keep cooking.

2 Stir in the yogurt, mint, chives, lemon zest, lemon juice, salt, and pepper. **Makes 1 cup**

PER ¼ CUP: 30 CALORIES, 0.2G TOTAL FAT (0G SATURATED), 1MG CHOLESTEROL, 0G DIETARY FIBER, 6G CARBOHYDRATE, 3G PROTEIN, 326MG SODIUM

Honey-Mustard Dipping Sauce

¼ cup Dijon mustard
3 tablespoons chopped cilantro
2 tablespoons fresh lemon juice
1 tablespoon honey
1 teaspoon ground coriander
½ teaspoon pepper

In a small bowl, stir together the mustard, cilantro, lemon juice, honey, coriander, and pepper. **Makes ½ cup**

PER 2 TABLESPOONS: 39 CALORIES, 1.5G TOTAL FAT (0.1G SATURATED), 0MG CHOLESTEROL, 1G DIETARY FIBER, 7G CARBOHYDRATE, 1G PROTEIN, 380MG SODIUM

Salmon with Braised Potatoes & Greens

Kale and Savoy cabbage are braised with garlic, apple, potatoes, and carrots to make a tender bed of vegetables for baked salmon.

F.Y.I.

Savoy cabbage is a good source of folate, and it also contains vitamin C and fiber; in addition, Savoy has more beta carotene than most other types of cabbage. Experimental studies show that the phytochemicals in cruciferous vegetables such as Savoy cabbage may fight cancer.

2 teaspoons olive oil
3 cloves garlic, minced
1 small Granny Smith apple, peeled and thinly sliced
¾ pound all-purpose potatoes, peeled and cut into ½-inch chunks
½ cup thinly sliced carrots
⅔ cup chicken broth, homemade (*page 32*) or reduced-sodium canned
3 cups shredded Savoy cabbage (about ½ pound)
2 cups shredded kale (about 4 ounces)
2 tablespoons balsamic vinegar
½ teaspoon salt
1¼ pounds salmon fillets, cut into 4 equal serving pieces

1 Preheat the oven to 425°. Spray a 7 x 11-inch baking pan with nonstick cooking spray.

2 In a large nonstick skillet, heat the oil over medium heat. Add the garlic and apple, and cook, stirring frequently, until the apple is golden, about 3 minutes.

3 Add the potatoes, carrots, and broth. Cover and simmer until the potatoes are almost tender, about 7 minutes.

4 Stir in the cabbage, kale, vinegar and ¼ teaspoon of the salt. Partially cover and cook until the cabbage has wilted and the potatoes are tender, about 10 minutes.

5 Meanwhile, place the salmon in the baking pan. Rub with the remaining ¼ teaspoon salt. Bake for 10 minutes, or until the salmon just flakes when tested with a fork. Serve the salmon on a bed of the braised vegetables.
Makes 4 servings

Scallops in Carrot-Vegetable Sauce

This scallop "stew" can be eaten on its own or served over a bowl of brown rice or noodles.

1½ cups carrot juice
1 large red bell pepper, diced
2 plum tomatoes, seeded and diced
2 shallots, minced
1 clove garlic, minced
¾ teaspoon salt
¼ teaspoon cayenne pepper
1¼ pounds sea scallops, halved horizontally
¾ cup frozen corn kernels, thawed
1½ teaspoons cornstarch blended with 1 tablespoon water

1 In a large skillet, combine the carrot juice, bell pepper, tomatoes, shallots, garlic, salt, and cayenne over medium heat. Bring to a boil, reduce to a simmer, cover, and cook 5 minutes.

2 Add the scallops and corn. Cover and cook until the scallops are just opaque, about 2 minutes. With a slotted spoon, transfer the scallops to a bowl.

3 Bring the carrot juice mixture in the skillet to a boil. Add the cornstarch mixture and cook, stirring, until slightly thickened, about 1 minute. Return the scallops to the pan and stir to coat with the sauce. ***Makes 4 servings***

Cod in Carrot-Vegetable Sauce Substitute 1¼ pounds skinless cod fillets cut into 1-inch chunks for the scallops. In step 2, add the cod and cook for 5 minutes before adding the corn. Continue with the recipe as above.

per serving	
calories	213
total fat	1.6g
saturated fat	0.2g
cholesterol	47mg
dietary fiber	3g
carbohydrate	24g
protein	26g
sodium	696mg

good source of: beta carotene, magnesium, potassium, selenium, vitamin B_{12}, vitamin B_6, vitamin C

KITCHEN *tip*

Fresh sea scallops should be glossy and firm, with a sweet smell; those with a strong odor of iodine or sulfur aren't fresh. Avoid unusually bright white scallops bulging at the sides; this may be a sign that they were soaked in water to increase their weight.

Moroccan-Style Fish Steaks

The spicy carrot juice mixture used to baste the fish steaks would also go well with any type of broiled poultry or pork tenderloin.

per serving	
calories	205
total fat	5.8g
saturated fat	0.8g
cholesterol	46mg
dietary fiber	1g
carbohydrate	6g
protein	31g
sodium	379mg

good source of: magnesium, niacin, omega-3 fatty acids, potassium, selenium, vitamin B_{12}, vitamin B_6

¼ cup carrot juice
4 teaspoons apricot all-fruit spread
2 teaspoons olive oil
1 teaspoon paprika
½ teaspoon salt
½ teaspoon cumin
½ teaspoon ground coriander
¼ teaspoon pepper
⅓ cup chopped cilantro
2 halibut steaks (10 ounces each), halved crosswise

1 In a small bowl, whisk together the carrot juice, fruit spread, oil, paprika, salt, cumin, coriander, and pepper. Stir in the cilantro.

2 Preheat the broiler. Place the halibut steaks on a broiler pan and brush with the carrot juice mixture. Broil 4 to 6 inches from the heat for 5 minutes, or until the top is browned and the flesh just flakes when tested with a fork. *Makes 4 servings*

Moroccan-Style Chicken Substitute 4 skinless, boneless chicken breasts (5 ounces each) for the halibut. In step 2, broil for 7 to 8 minutes, or until the chicken is cooked through.

Salmon-Potato Loaf

The grated lemon zest and lemon juice are the perfect counterpoint to the rich flavor of the salmon. If you like, serve lemon wedges with the salmon loaf.

per serving	
calories	299
total fat	7.3g
saturated fat	1.8g
cholesterol	58mg
dietary fiber	5g
carbohydrate	31g
protein	28g
sodium	955mg

good source of: beta carotene, calcium, folate, magnesium, niacin, omega-3 fatty acids, potassium, riboflavin, selenium, vitamin B_{12}, vitamin B_6, vitamin C, vitamin D

1 pound baking potatoes, peeled and thinly sliced
3 cloves garlic, slivered
½ teaspoon salt
1 can (14¾ ounces) pink salmon (not drained)
1 package (10 ounces) frozen chopped spinach, thawed and squeezed dry
½ cup quick-cooking oats
3 scallions, thinly sliced
2 teaspoons grated lemon zest
3 tablespoons fresh lemon juice
2 large egg whites

1 Preheat the oven to 350°F. Spray an 8½ x 4½-inch loaf pan with nonstick cooking spray.

2 Bring a large pot of water to a boil. Add the potatoes and garlic. Reduce to a simmer and cook until the potatoes are tender, about 7 minutes. Drain, reserving ¼ cup of the potato cooking liquid. Transfer the potatoes and garlic to a large bowl and mash with a potato masher.

3 Add the reserved potato cooking liquid, the salt, salmon, spinach, oats, scallions, lemon zest, lemon juice, and egg whites to the mashed potatoes. Mix well, breaking up the salmon and any bones (leave them in).

4 Spoon the mixture into the loaf pan, smoothing the top. Bake 35 minutes, or until a toothpick inserted in the center of the loaf comes out clean. Cool in the pan for 15 minutes before inverting onto a serving platter. Serve warm or chilled. ***Makes 4 servings***

F.Y.I.

Along with the heart-healthy omega-3 fatty acids found in canned salmon, you will get an additional boost of calcium by eating the bones, which are softened and delicate, making them entirely edible. The average amount of calcium in ½ cup of canned salmon with the bones is 290 mg—almost equivalent to 1 cup of milk, which has 300mg calcium. While calcium helps prevent osteoporosis, some studies also show that getting enough calcium may also help lower blood pressure.

Bluefish with Spicy Orange-Tomato Sauce

Substitute halibut, grouper, tuna, or other meaty fish if you like.

ON THE *Menu*

This bluefish dish yields a fair amount of sauce, so it would be delicious served over a mound of brown rice. On the side, serve steamed asparagus and a salad of baby spinach with a squeeze of lemon juice. For dessert, serve chilled cantaloupe wedges with a dipping sauce of fat-free sour cream and brown sugar.

> 2 teaspoons olive oil
> 1 large green bell pepper, diced
> 1 large carrot, diced
> 3 cloves garlic, minced
> 1 tablespoon minced fresh ginger
> 1½ cups spicy tomato-vegetable juice
> ½ teaspoon grated orange zest
> 3 tablespoons orange juice
> ½ teaspoon thyme
> 4 skinless bluefish fillets (6 ounces each)

1 In a large nonstick skillet, heat the oil over medium heat. Add the bell pepper, carrot, garlic, and ginger, and cook, stirring frequently, until the vegetables have softened, about 7 minutes.

2 Stir in the tomato-vegetable juice, orange zest, orange juice, and thyme, and bring to a boil. Reduce to a simmer and place the bluefish fillets on top. Spoon some of the sauce over the fish, cover, and cook until the fish just flakes when tested with a fork, about 10 minutes.

3 Transfer the fish to serving plates and top with the vegetables and sauce. *Makes 4 servings*

Spotlite recipe

Cooking food in a sealed packet (en papillote) is one of the best ways to preserve nutrients and use a minimum of fat. The traditional method is to cook the food in a packet made of parchment paper. A square sheet of cooking parchment is folded in half and trimmed to a shape similar to half a heart. A simpler method is to use aluminum foil, as described in this salmon recipe. For a chicken dish cooked en papillote, see page 77.

Salmon en Papillote

⅓ cup water
4 cloves garlic, minced
½ pound shiitake mushrooms, stems discarded and
   caps thinly sliced
1 package (10 ounces) frozen chopped spinach, thawed
   and squeezed dry
¾ teaspoon salt
½ teaspoon rosemary, minced
1 can (15 ounces) cannellini beans, rinsed and drained
¼ cup fresh lemon juice
4 skinless salmon fillets (5 ounces each)

1 Preheat the oven to 450°F. In a large nonstick skillet, heat the water over medium heat. Add the garlic and cook until tender, about 3 minutes. Add the mushrooms, spinach, ¼ teaspoon of the salt, and the rosemary, and cook until the mushrooms are tender, about 5 minutes. Transfer the mixture to a large bowl. Stir in the beans and 2 tablespoons of the lemon juice.

2 Cut four pieces of foil 12 x 18 inches each. With the short end of the foil facing you, spoon the spinach-bean mixture onto the bottom half of each sheet, leaving a 2-inch border around the edges. Top each mound with a salmon fillet. Sprinkle the salmon with the remaining 2 tablespoons lemon juice and ½ teaspoon salt.

3 Fold the foil over the vegetables and fish, folding the edges over to seal. Place the packets on a baking sheet and bake 10 minutes, or until the fish is cooked through. Carefully open one package (be careful—steam will escape) and check for doneness. If the fish isn't done, reseal the packet and return the baking sheet to the oven. *Makes 4 servings*

PER SERVING **295 calories, 5.5g total fat (0.9g saturated), 74mg cholesterol, 7g dietary fiber, 26g carbohydrate, 37g protein, 764mg sodium**
Good source of: **beta carotene, folate, magnesium, niacin, omega-3 fatty acids, potassium, selenium, thiamin, vitamin B$_{12}$, vitamin B$_6$, vitamin C, vitamin D**

Broiled Tuna Burgers

While tuna burgers are often made by combining tuna with breadcrumbs, we've used heart-healthy oats instead. The sun-dried tomato "bits" can be found in many supermarkets. If all you can find are whole sun-dried tomato halves, choose soft, tender tomatoes and cut them into bits with a pair of scissors or a knife.

> 2 cans (6 ounces each) water-packed albacore tuna,
>   drained
> ¼ cup plain fat-free yogurt
> 2 tablespoons light mayonnaise
> ¼ cup sun-dried tomato bits (not oil-packed)
> 3 scallions, thinly sliced
> 3 tablespoons quick-cooking oats

1 In a large bowl, combine the tuna, yogurt, mayonnaise, sun-dried tomatoes, scallions, and oats. Stir until well combined.

2 Preheat the broiler. Spray a broiler pan with nonstick cooking spray. Shape the tuna mixture into 4 patties. Broil 4 to 6 inches from the heat for 3 to 4 minutes per side, or until crusty and heated through. ***Makes 4 servings***

Broiled Salmon Burgers Substitute 1 can (14¾ ounces) pink salmon, drained, for the tuna. Increase the yogurt to ⅓ cup and reduce the mayonnaise to 1 tablespoon.

ON THE *Menu*

Serve the tuna burgers on toasted sourdough English muffins. On the side, serve finely shredded carrots and scallions tossed with fat-free ranch dressing. For dessert, serve Strawberry-Rhubarb Compote (*page 125*).

Baked Fish Fillets with Oat & Nut Crust

Tilapia is a firm, white-fleshed fish with a meaty flavor. You could also make this with snapper or grouper.

½ cup old-fashioned rolled oats
2 tablespoons walnut pieces
1 teaspoon grated orange zest
½ teaspoon fennel seeds
½ teaspoon salt
4 skinless tilapia fillets (5 ounces each)
2 large egg whites beaten with 1 tablespoon water

1 Preheat the oven to 450°F. Spray a large baking sheet with nonstick cooking spray. In a food processor, combine the oats, walnuts, orange zest, fennel seeds, and salt, and pulse the machine on and off until the oats are coarsely ground. Transfer to a large shallow bowl.

2 Dip the tilapia fillets in the egg white mixture, then in the oat mixture, patting it into the fish. Place the fish on the baking sheet and spray the fish with nonstick cooking spray. Bake for 10 minutes, or until the coating is lightly browned and crisp, and the fish just flakes when tested with a fork.
Makes 4 servings

ON THE Menu

Serve the snapper with brown rice and Two-Pea Sauté (*page 112*). For dessert, crumble amaretti (Italian macaroons) over applesauce.

Orange-Broiled Snapper

If you don't feel like making one of the sauces to go with this broiled fish, you can simply serve it with a squeeze of fresh lemon juice—or even a splash of fat-free salad dressing.

Lemon-Herb Dipping Sauce or Honey-Mustard
   Dipping Sauce (*both on page 43*)
¼ cup orange juice
2 teaspoons olive oil
½ teaspoon sugar
½ teaspoon salt
½ teaspoon oregano
¼ teaspoon cayenne pepper
4 skin-on red snapper fillets (5 ounces each)

1 Prepare one of the dipping sauces. Divide the sauce among 4 small serving bowls and refrigerate until serving time.

2 Preheat the broiler. In a small bowl, whisk together the orange juice, oil, sugar, salt, oregano, and cayenne.

3 Place the fillets, skin-side down, on a broiler pan. Brush the orange juice mixture over the fish and broil 4 to 6 inches from the heat for 5 minutes, or until the snapper just flakes when tested with a fork. Serve with a bowl of sauce for each person. Remove the skin before eating. ***Makes 4 servings***

Lemon-Broiled Snapper Substitute lemon juice for the orange juice, but use only 3 tablespoons.

per serving	
calories	468
total fat	6.9g
saturated fat	1.6g
cholesterol	50mg
dietary fiber	5g
carbohydrate	73g
protein	28g
sodium	451mg

good source of: niacin, riboflavin, selenium, thiamin, vitamin B$_6$, vitamin C

F.Y.I.

Five-spice powder is a pungent ground spice mixture often used in Chinese cooking. Cinnamon, cloves, fennel seed, star anise, and Szechuan peppercorns are the traditional components. It's available in many supermarkets and in Asian markets. If you can't find it, you can make your own: In a spice grinder, finely grind 2 tablespoons each of Szechuan peppercorns, star anise, and fennel seeds. Stir in 2 tablespoons each of ground cinnamon and ground cloves. Makes about ½ cup.

Chinese Roast Pork Salad

If you're preparing this in the summer, and have access to a grill, by all means barbecue the pork instead of roasting it.

¼ cup plum preserves or apricot jam
3 tablespoons reduced-sodium soy sauce
1 teaspoon Chinese five-spice powder
½ teaspoon ground ginger
2 tablespoons rice vinegar
2 teaspoons dark sesame oil
¾ pound pork tenderloin
8 ounces capellini (angel-hair) pasta, broken in half
½ pound snow peas, strings removed
2 red apples (6 ounces each), unpeeled and cut into
    ½-inch chunks
4 scallions, thinly sliced
6 cups shredded romaine lettuce

1 Preheat the oven to 450°F. In a large bowl, combine the preserves, soy sauce, five-spice powder, and ginger. Measure out 2 tablespoons of the soy sauce mixture and set aside to use for brushing on the pork. Add the vinegar and sesame oil to the soy sauce mixture remaining in the bowl.

2 Place the pork in a foil-lined baking pan and brush the reserved 2 tablespoons soy sauce mixture over the pork. Roast for 30 minutes, or until the meat is cooked through but still juicy.

3 Meanwhile, in a large pot of boiling water, cook the pasta according to package directions. Add the snow peas for the last 30 seconds of cooking time. Drain the pasta and snow peas and add to the bowl with the dressing.

4 When the pork is cool enough to handle, cut it into ¼ x 2-inch strips and add them to the bowl. Add the apples and scallions. Toss well.

5 Serve the salad at room temperature or chilled, on a bed of shredded romaine lettuce. ***Makes 4 servings***

Heart-Smart Meatloaf

Lean ground turkey breast replaces some of the beef in this loaf, and lentils and oats add cholesterol-lowering soluble fiber. Serve the loaf hot or cold.

2 teaspoons olive oil
1 large onion, finely chopped
1 carrot, finely chopped
3 cloves garlic, minced
½ cup red lentils
1⅓ cups water
1 teaspoon salt
¾ teaspoon thyme
½ pound top round beef, cut into chunks
¼ pound skinless, boneless turkey breast, cut into chunks
⅓ cup old-fashioned rolled oats
2 large egg whites
¼ cup no-salt-added ketchup
1 teaspoon reduced-sodium soy sauce

1 Preheat the oven to 350°F. Spray an 8½ x 4½-inch loaf pan with nonstick cooking spray.

2 In a medium nonstick saucepan, heat the oil over low heat. Add the onion, carrot, and garlic, and cook, stirring frequently, until the onion is tender, about 10 minutes. Stir in the lentils, water, ¼ teaspoon of the salt, and the thyme. Bring to a boil and cook until the lentils are tender, 7 to 10 minutes. Transfer the lentil mixture (including any liquid remaining in the pan) to a large bowl and let cool to room temperature.

3 In a food processor, pulse the beef and turkey until finely ground. Add to the bowl with the lentils.

4 Add the remaining ¾ teaspoon salt, the oats, and egg whites, stirring until well combined. Spoon the meatloaf mixture into the loaf pan. Bake for 30 minutes.

5 Meanwhile, in a small bowl, stir together the ketchup and soy sauce. After the meatloaf has baked for 30 minutes, brush the ketchup mixture over the top of the loaf. Bake 5 minutes longer, or until the juices run clear when a toothpick is inserted into the loaf. Let sit 10 minutes before slicing. ***Makes 4 servings***

Picadillo with Lentils

Picadillo, which means "mince" in Spanish, is the Latin American version of hash. It varies with the region, but invariably contains chopped meat (usually pork, beef, or veal), and often tomatoes. Raisins are also a fairly common ingredient in the Cuban rendition of this dish. Our slimmed-down version is made with lean pork tenderloin and folate-rich lentils.

1 tablespoon olive oil
1 green bell pepper, diced
3 cloves garlic, slivered
1 pound pork tenderloin, cut into chunks
1 cup lentils, picked over and rinsed
1 can (14½ ounces) no-salt-added stewed tomatoes
1 can (15 ounces) crushed tomatoes
1 cup water
⅓ cup raisins
¼ cup pimiento-stuffed olives, coarsely chopped
½ teaspoon salt
¼ teaspoon cayenne pepper

1 In a nonstick Dutch oven, heat the oil over medium heat. Add the bell pepper and garlic, and cook until the pepper is tender, about 5 minutes.

2 Meanwhile, in a food processor, pulse the pork until coarsely ground. Add the pork to the pan and cook until no longer pink, about 4 minutes.

3 Add the lentils, stewed tomatoes, crushed tomatoes, water, raisins, olives, salt, and cayenne. Bring to a boil, reduce to a simmer, cover, and cook until the lentils are tender, about 25 minutes. ***Makes 4 servings***

Vegetarian Picadillo Omit the pork and increase the lentils to 1¼ cups. Instead of water (added in step 3), use carrot juice and increase the amount to 1¼ cups.

per serving	
calories	454
total fat	9g
saturated fat	2g
cholesterol	74mg
dietary fiber	20g
carbohydrate	55g
protein	41g
sodium	654mg

good source of: fiber, folate, iron, magnesium, niacin, potassium, riboflavin, selenium, thiamin, vitamin B_{12}, vitamin B_6, vitamin C, zinc

F.Y.I.

An inexpensive, low-fat source of fiber, protein, iron, potassium, and zinc, the lentil is also a good source of B vitamins, including heart-healthy folate. For example, a mere ½ cup of cooked lentils will supply about half of your daily requirement for this B vitamin.

marinades

Marinades work to provide tenderness as well as flavor to meat, poultry, fish, and soft vegetables. Place the ingredients to be marinated in a sturdy zip-seal plastic bag and pour in the marinade. Marinate in the refrigerator for at least 30 minutes or up to overnight. Lift the marinated ingredient from the plastic bag, reserving the marinade for basting. Baste the ingredient with the marinade as it cooks (by broiling, grilling, baking, or roasting). When the marinade is being used on poultry, meat, or fish, there are some things you should do to avoid any potential foodborne bacteria being introduced into the marinade with the basting brush: 1) don't brush with any marinade during the final 5 minutes of cooking time, and 2) never serve any leftover marinade as a sauce.

These marinades yield enough to coat from 1 to 1½ pounds of an ingredient.

Thai-Style Marinade

⅓ cup reduced-sodium soy sauce

¼ cup fresh lime juice

1 tablespoon sugar

3 tablespoons chopped fresh mint or basil

3 tablespoons chopped cilantro

2 cloves garlic, minced

In a jar with a tight-fitting lid, combine all of the ingredients and shake until well blended. Store in the refrigerator. *Makes ¾ cup*

PER 3 TABLESPOONS: 44 CALORIES, 0.1G TOTAL FAT (0G SATURATED), 0MG CHOLESTEROL, 0G DIETARY FIBER, 10G CARBOHYDRATE, 1G PROTEIN, 707MG SODIUM

Pineapple-Ginger Marinade

½ cup frozen pineapple juice concentrate, thawed

2 tablespoons reduced-sodium soy sauce

2 cloves garlic, minced

1 tablespoon minced fresh ginger

2 teaspoons dark sesame oil

½ teaspoon salt

In a jar with a tight-fitting lid, combine all of the ingredients and shake until well blended. Store in the refrigerator. *Makes ¾ cup*

PER 3 TABLESPOONS: 93 CALORIES, 2.4G TOTAL FAT (0.4G SATURATED), 0MG CHOLESTEROL, 0G DIETARY FIBER, 17G CARBOHYDRATE, 1G PROTEIN, 559MG SODIUM. **GOOD SOURCE OF:** VITAMIN C

Chipotle-Garlic Marinade

½ cup no-salt-added ketchup

2 tablespoons cider vinegar

1 tablespoon plus 1½ teaspoons chipotle hot sauce

2½ teaspoons honey

1½ teaspoons chili powder

½ teaspoon salt

4 cloves garlic, minced

In a jar with a tight-fitting lid, combine all of the ingredients and shake until well blended. Store in the refrigerator. *Makes ¾ cup*

PER 3 TABLESPOONS: 53 CALORIES, 0.3G TOTAL FAT (0.1G SATURATED), 0MG CHOLESTEROL, 1G DIETARY FIBER, 14G CARBOHYDRATE, 1G PROTEIN, 309MG SODIUM

Pork & Beans

per serving	
calories	296
total fat	4.8g
saturated fat	1.1g
cholesterol	37mg
dietary fiber	10g
carbohydrate	43g
protein	20g
sodium	495mg

good source of: beta carotene, fiber, folate, potassium, selenium, thiamin, vitamin B$_6$, vitamin C

Tomatoes, carrot juice, molasses, and ground ginger add up to an intriguing mixture of sweet, spicy, and pungent. This combination works especially well with the richness of pork and the creaminess of pinto beans. For a vegetarian version of pork and beans, see No Pork Baked Beans (*page 115*).

2 teaspoons olive oil
1 large onion, finely chopped
1 red bell pepper, diced
3 cloves garlic, minced
½ pound pork tenderloin, cut into ½-inch chunks
1 can (14½ ounces) no-salt-added stewed tomatoes
¾ cup carrot juice
2 tablespoons light molasses
1 teaspoon ground ginger
½ teaspoon salt
1 can (19 ounces) pinto beans, rinsed and drained

1 In a large nonstick saucepan or Dutch oven, heat the oil over medium heat. Add the onion, bell pepper, and garlic, and cook, stirring frequently, until the onion is golden brown, about 7 minutes.

2 Add the pork and cook until no longer pink, about 5 minutes.

3 Stir in the tomatoes, carrot juice, molasses, ginger, and salt, and bring to a boil. Add the beans, reduce to a simmer, cover, and cook 15 minutes.

4 Uncover and cook until the pork is tender, about 10 minutes. *Makes 4 servings*

Mexican Pork & Beans Substitute 4 sliced scallions for the onion. Omit the red bell pepper and use 1 green bell pepper and 1 pickled jalapeño pepper, diced, instead. Replace the pinto beans with black beans and add 1 cup of corn kernels when you add the beans.

Beef, Shiitake & Pasta Stir-Fry

If you have leftover pasta or rice on hand (you'll need about 3 cups), use it here in place of the fresh cooked ditalini.

per serving	
calories	314
total fat	9.8g
saturated fat	2.5g
cholesterol	48mg
dietary fiber	4g
carbohydrate	35g
protein	22g
sodium	361mg

good source of: beta carotene, niacin, riboflavin, selenium, vitamin B_{12}, vitamin B_6, vitamin D, zinc

1 cup ditalini pasta or small pasta shells
10 ounces well-trimmed beef sirloin, cut into thin strips
2 tablespoons plus 2 teaspoons cornstarch
2 teaspoons olive oil
½ pound fresh shiitake mushrooms, stems discarded and caps quartered
2 carrots, cut into matchsticks
3 cloves garlic, minced
1 tablespoon minced fresh ginger
2 cups halved cherry tomatoes
2 tablespoons reduced-sodium soy sauce
2 teaspoons dark sesame oil
½ teaspoon light brown sugar
¼ teaspoon crushed red pepper flakes

1 In a large saucepan of boiling water, cook the pasta until just barely tender. Drain.

2 Meanwhile, dredge the beef in 2 tablespoons of the cornstarch, shaking off the excess. In a large nonstick wok or skillet, heat the olive oil over medium heat. Add the beef and cook, stirring frequently, until browned, about 3 minutes. With a slotted spoon, transfer the beef to a plate and set aside.

3 Add the mushrooms, carrots, garlic, and ginger to the pan. Cook, stirring frequently, until the carrot is crisp-tender, about 3 minutes. Stir in the cherry tomatoes, soy sauce, sesame oil, brown sugar, and red pepper flakes. Increase the heat to medium-high and bring to a boil.

4 In a cup, stir together the remaining 2 teaspoons cornstarch and 3 tablespoons of water. Stir the cornstarch mixture and drained pasta into the skillet. Cook, stirring constantly, until the mixture is slightly thickened, about 2 minutes. Return the beef to the pan and cook until heated through, about 1 minute. *Makes 4 servings*

F.Y.I.

Among their many other nutritional virtues, sweet potatoes are a good source of vitamin E. This is notable because the sweet potato is a low-fat source of this vitamin, which is usually found in high-fat foods such as oils and nuts.

Barbecued Pork & Mashed Sweet Potatoes

The slight sweetness of the glaze on the pork is underscored by the natural sweetness of the sweet potatoes.

⅓ cup ketchup
1 tablespoon red wine vinegar
1 tablespoon honey
1½ teaspoons chili powder
½ teaspoon ground ginger
1 pound pork tenderloin
¾ teaspoon salt
1½ pounds sweet potatoes, peeled and thinly sliced
6 cloves garlic, slivered

1 Preheat the oven to 425°F.

2 In a small bowl, combine the ketchup, vinegar, honey, chili powder, and ginger. Measure out 2 tablespoons of the ketchup mixture and set aside to use in step 6, with the sweet potatoes.

3 Spray a roasting pan with nonstick cooking spray. Place the pork in the pan and sprinkle with ¼ teaspoon of the salt. Bake 10 minutes.

4 Brush the pork with half of the ketchup mixture in the small bowl, and bake 10 minutes. Brush with the remaining ketchup mixture in the bowl and bake until the pork is cooked through and richly browned, about 10 minutes longer.

5 Meanwhile, in a medium saucepan, combine the sweet potatoes, garlic, and water to cover, and bring to a boil over medium heat. Reduce to a simmer and cook until the sweet potatoes are tender, about 10 minutes. Drain.

6 With a potato masher, mash the sweet potatoes with the remaining ½ teaspoon salt and the reserved 2 tablespoons of ketchup mixture until smooth. Thinly slice the pork just before serving. ***Makes 4 servings***

Southwestern Beef Hash

The word hash comes from the French verb *hâcher*, which means "to chop." So a hash is always a dish of chopped or cut-up ingredients cooked together. Here, roast beef hash gets a healthy helping of vegetables and Southwestern seasonings. (*For a Latin American-style hash made with pork, see Picadillo with Lentils, page 55.*)

per serving	
calories	329
total fat	8g
saturated fat	2g
cholesterol	33mg
dietary fiber	6g
carbohydrate	50g
protein	17g
sodium	584mg

good source of: beta carotene, niacin, potassium, vitamin B$_{12}$, vitamin B$_6$, vitamin C, zinc

½ teaspoon salt
¾ pound red potatoes, cut into ½-inch chunks
½ pound sweet potatoes, peeled and cut into ½-inch chunks
1 tablespoon olive oil
1 medium onion, finely chopped
1 large red bell pepper, finely diced
3 cloves garlic, minced
1 package (10 ounces) frozen corn kernels, thawed
6 ounces sliced lean roast beef, cut into ½-inch strips
2 teaspoons chili powder

1 Bring a large pot of water to a boil. Add ¼ teaspoon of the salt, the red potatoes, and sweet potatoes, and cook until the potatoes are tender, about 7 minutes. Drain well.

2 Meanwhile, in a large nonstick skillet, heat the oil over medium heat. Add the onion, bell pepper, and garlic, and cook until the onion is tender, about 7 minutes.

3 Add the drained potatoes, stirring to combine. Add the remaining ¼ teaspoon salt, the corn, beef, and chili powder, and cook, turning the potatoes occasionally, until the potatoes are lightly golden, about 7 minutes. ***Makes 4 servings***

Southwestern Red Flannel Hash Stir in 1 can (16 ounces) drained diced beets when adding the corn.

Green Chili with Pork & Hominy

The stew called chili comes in two basic colors: red and green. Very generally speaking, red chilis are tomato-based and are made with beef. Green chilis, on the other hand, are made with pork and get their green color from green peppers. Hominy is also a common ingredient in green chilis.

per serving	
calories	288
total fat	8.4g
saturated fat	2g
cholesterol	74mg
dietary fiber	4g
carbohydrate	25g
protein	27g
sodium	721mg

good source of: niacin, riboflavin, selenium, thiamin, vitamin B_{12}, vitamin B_6, vitamin C, zinc

¾ pound pork tenderloin, cut into ½-inch chunks
2 tablespoons flour
1 tablespoon olive oil
1 medium onion, finely chopped
1 green bell pepper, diced
3 cloves garlic, minced
½ cup water
1 cup chicken broth, homemade (*page 32*) or reduced-sodium canned
⅔ cup chopped cilantro
1 teaspoon jalapeño pepper sauce
½ teaspoon salt
1 can (15 ounces) white hominy, rinsed and drained
1 tablespoon fresh lime juice

1 Dredge the pork in the flour, shaking off the excess. In a nonstick Dutch oven, heat the oil over medium-high heat. Add the pork and sauté until golden brown, about 5 minutes. With a slotted spoon, transfer the pork to a plate.

2 Reduce the heat to medium. Stir in the onion, bell pepper, garlic, and water, scraping up any browned bits clinging to the bottom of the pan. Cook until the onion is tender, about 7 minutes.

3 Add the broth, ⅓ cup of the cilantro, the jalapeño pepper sauce, and the salt, and bring to a boil. Add the pork and hominy, reduce to a simmer, cover, and cook until the pork is cooked through, about 5 minutes.

4 Stir in the remaining ⅓ cup cilantro and the lime juice and serve. ***Makes 4 servings***

F.Y.I.

Hominy is large, dried white or yellow corn kernels with the hull and germ removed. Traditionally this is done by soaking the corn in a solution of lime (or lye) and water to loosen the skin. Although removing the hull can also be accomplished mechanically, it's the lime or lye solution that gives the Southwestern and Mexican versions of hominy, called *posole*, their distinctive flavor. It is not that common to find whole, dried hominy.

Crispy Deviled Chicken

The mustard-horseradish mixture (in step 1) can also be made on its own and used to perk up cooked vegetables.

> 3 tablespoons Dijon mustard
> 2 tablespoons drained white horseradish
> 2 teaspoons fresh lemon juice
> ½ teaspoon hot pepper sauce
> ½ teaspoon rosemary, minced
> ¼ cup plain dried breadcrumbs
> ¼ cup quick-cooking oats
> 2 teaspoons paprika
> 4 small skinless, boneless chicken breast halves
>   (4 ounces each)

1 Preheat the broiler. In a small bowl, stir together the mustard, horseradish, lemon juice, hot pepper sauce, and rosemary until well combined.

2 In a small bowl, stir together the breadcrumbs, oats, and paprika. Place the chicken on the broiler pan and brush with half the mustard-horseradish mixture. Sprinkle half the breadcrumb mixture over the chicken and pat it on. Spray the chicken with nonstick cooking spray.

3 Broil 4 to 6 inches from the heat for 4 minutes. Turn the chicken over and brush with the remaining mustard-horseradish mixture and coat with the remaining breadcrumb mixture. Spray with nonstick cooking spray. Broil for 3 minutes, or until the chicken is cooked through and the crumbs are golden brown and crispy. *Makes 4 servings*

Chicken Caesar Toss sliced hearts of romaine lettuce with low-fat or fat-free caesar dressing and top with the deviled chicken, cut into strips.

per serving	
calories	207
total fat	5g
saturated fat	1.1g
cholesterol	72mg
dietary fiber	1g
carbohydrate	11g
protein	29g
sodium	433mg

good source of: niacin, selenium, vitamin B$_6$

KITCHEN*tip*

If you don't have quick-cooking oats on hand, make your own from old-fashioned rolled oats. Place the oats in a food processor and pulse it on and off until the oats are finely ground, but not powdery.

Turkey Tetrazzini

Although turkey tetrazzini is traditionally baked, you can omit the final step and simply toss the hot pasta and shredded turkey with the sauce and serve.

8 ounces whole-wheat penne or fusilli
1½ cups chicken broth, homemade (*page 32*) or
    reduced-sodium canned
1 cup low-fat (1%) milk
3 tablespoons flour
1 red bell pepper, cut into ½-inch squares
½ pound fresh shiitake mushrooms, stems discarded and
    caps thinly sliced
¼ teaspoon salt
¼ teaspoon cayenne pepper
½ pound cooked turkey breast, shredded (2 cups)
¼ cup grated Parmesan cheese

1 Preheat the oven to 400°F. In a large pot of boiling water, cook the pasta according to package directions. Drain, reserving ⅓ cup of the pasta cooking water.

2 Meanwhile, in a large saucepan, whisk the broth and the milk into the flour until smooth. Stir in the bell pepper, mushrooms, salt, and cayenne. Cook over medium heat, stirring constantly, until the sauce is slightly thickened and the bell pepper is tender, about 5 minutes.

3 Transfer the sauce to a large bowl and add the drained pasta, reserved pasta cooking water, turkey, and Parmesan.

4 Transfer to a 7 x 11-inch baking dish. Bake 15 minutes, or until the pasta is piping hot and the top is crusty. ***Makes 4 servings***

Curried Smoked Turkey Salad

With a little judicious doctoring, you can turn a storebought salad dressing into something interesting and "homemade." We've started with a honey-mustard dressing, but you could also try this recipe with a fat-free ranch dressing. If you use the ranch dressing, increase the amount to ¾ cup and omit the sour cream. The amount of curry powder stays the same.

⅔ cup bottled fat-free honey-mustard dressing
2 tablespoons fat-free sour cream
2 teaspoons curry powder
1 cup raisins
1 package (12 ounces) romaine lettuce hearts, cut into
   bite-size pieces
½ pound sliced smoked turkey, cut into ½-inch-wide
   strips
¼ cup coarsely chopped walnuts, pecans, or cashews

1 In a large bowl, whisk together the dressing, sour cream, and curry powder. Add the raisins and toss to combine.

2 Add the lettuce, turkey, and walnuts, and toss again. ***Makes 4 servings***

PER SERVING **271 calories, 6.1g total fat (0.8g saturated), 25mg cholesterol, 5g dietary fiber, 44g carbohydrate, 15g protein, 668mg sodium**
Good source of: **folate, potassium, vitamin C**

per serving	
calories	215
total fat	6.1g
saturated fat	1.5g
cholesterol	74mg
dietary fiber	2g
carbohydrate	10g
protein	29g
sodium	385mg

good source of: niacin, selenium, vitamin B_6, vitamin C

KITCHEN tip

If you use wooden skewers for grilling or broiling, soak them in water before using them so they won't burn. Place them in a pan of water and let them soak for at least 30 minutes before you are ready to grill.

Chicken Kebabs with Minted Yogurt Sauce

If you like, make a double batch of the minted yogurt sauce and toss it with boiled potatoes for a side dish.

½ cup plain low-fat yogurt
⅓ cup chopped fresh mint
½ teaspoon grated lemon zest
½ teaspoon salt
½ teaspoon pepper
3 tablespoons fresh lemon juice
2 teaspoons olive oil
2 cloves garlic, minced
1 teaspoon oregano
1 pound skinless, boneless chicken breast, cut into
    16 chunks
1 red onion, cut into 16 chunks
16 cherry tomatoes

1 In a small bowl, combine the yogurt, mint, lemon zest, ¼ teaspoon of the salt, and ¼ teaspoon of the pepper. Cover and refrigerate until serving time.

2 In a shallow bowl, combine the lemon juice, oil, garlic, oregano, remaining ¼ teaspoon salt, and ¼ teaspoon pepper. Add the chicken and onion, tossing to coat.

3 Preheat the broiler. Alternately thread the chicken, onion, and cherry tomatoes onto 8 skewers. Broil the kebabs, turning occasionally, for 8 minutes, or until the chicken is cooked through. Serve with the minted yogurt sauce. ***Makes 4 servings***

Broiled Chicken & Macaroni Salad Double the amount of yogurt-mint sauce. Cook 8 ounces of elbow macaroni, drain, and rinse under cold running water. Broil the kebabs as directed. Remove the broiled ingredients from the skewers and toss with the cooked pasta and yogurt-mint sauce. Serve at room temperature or chilled.

F.Y.I.

Porcini mushrooms have a woodsy, almost meaty flavor. Not that easy to come by in their fresh form, they are readily available in gourmet stores and Italian markets in their dried form. Like other dried mushrooms, they need to be reconstituted in hot water before they are used; the soaking water is often incorporated into the dish.

Chicken, Broccoli & Porcini with Fettuccine

Both dried and fresh mushrooms are the base for this sauce.

½ cup dried porcini or other dried mushrooms (½ ounce)
½ cup boiling water
3 teaspoons olive oil
6 ounces skinless, boneless chicken breast, cut into strips
½ pound fresh button mushrooms, quartered
1¼ cups tomato-vegetable juice
¾ teaspoon salt
½ teaspoon sage
½ teaspoon pepper
5 cups small broccoli florets
1 teaspoon cornstarch blended with 1 tablespoon water
8 ounces whole-wheat fettuccine

1 In a small heatproof bowl, combine the porcini and boiling water; let stand for 20 minutes to soften. Reserving the soaking liquid, scoop out the porcini and coarsely chop. Strain the liquid through a fine-mesh sieve.

2 Meanwhile, in a large nonstick skillet, heat 2 teaspoons of the oil over medium heat. Add the chicken and cook until golden brown, about 4 minutes. With a slotted spoon, transfer to a plate.

3 Add the remaining 1 teaspoon oil and fresh mushrooms to the skillet and cook, stirring frequently, until the mushrooms are lightly colored, about 4 minutes. Stir in the tomato-vegetable juice, salt, sage, and pepper. Add the chopped porcini and mushroom soaking liquid to the skillet. Bring the mushroom sauce to a boil. Add the broccoli and chicken. Reduce to a simmer, cover, and cook until the broccoli is tender and the chicken is cooked through, about 3 minutes.

4 Stir the cornstarch mixture into the skillet, bring to a boil over medium heat and cook until slightly thickened, about 1 minute. Transfer the sauce to a large serving bowl.

5 In large pot of boiling water, cook the pasta according to package directions. Drain, reserving ½ cup of the cooking water. Add the fettuccine and reserved cooking water to the serving bowl and toss to combine. **Makes 4 servings**

Indian-Style Turkey Burgers

These tempting turkey burgers are flavored with mango chutney, yogurt, and curry powder—common ingredients in Indian cuisine. The burgers can be shaped ahead of time and refrigerated for several hours. The chutney topping (step 2) can also be made ahead.

per serving	
calories	316
total fat	8.1g
saturated fat	2.6g
cholesterol	56mg
dietary fiber	6g
carbohydrate	43g
protein	20g
sodium	936mg

good source of:
niacin, selenium, thiamin, vitamin B₆

¾ pound lean ground turkey
¼ cup plain dried breadcrumbs
¼ cup mango chutney, finely chopped
3 tablespoons ketchup
2 tablespoons plain fat-free yogurt
2 teaspoons Dijon mustard
1½ teaspoons curry powder
¼ teaspoon salt
4 whole-wheat English muffins, split and toasted
1 cup mixed greens

1   In a medium bowl, combine the turkey, breadcrumbs, 2 tablespoons of the chutney, 1 tablespoon of the ketchup, the yogurt, mustard, 1 teaspoon of the curry powder, and the salt. Mix well and shape into 4 patties.

2   In a small bowl, combine the remaining 2 tablespoons chutney, 2 tablespoons ketchup, and ½ teaspoon curry powder.

3   Preheat the broiler. Cook the burgers 4 to 6 inches from the heat for 6 minutes, turning once, until browned and cooked through. Serve the burgers on the English muffins topped with the chutney mixture and greens.
Makes 4 servings

KITCHEN *tip*

An enzyme in kiwifruits, called actinidin, breaks down protein. Therefore, when combining kiwis with chicken (as in this recipe), the two ingredients should not be allowed to sit together for more than 1 or 2 hours, or the actinidin will turn the chicken mushy.

Chicken Salad with Kiwi & Honey-Lime Dressing

Once an expensive imported fruit, the beautiful green kiwifruit is now grown extensively in this country.

> ¾ pound skinless, boneless chicken breasts
> 2 teaspoons grated lime zest
> ¼ cup fresh lime juice
> 2 tablespoons honey
> 2 tablespoons reduced-sodium soy sauce
> ½ teaspoon ground ginger
> 8 cups (loosely packed) shredded romaine lettuce
> 2 kiwifruit, peeled, halved lengthwise, and thinly sliced crosswise
> ½ cup canned sliced water chestnuts, rinsed and drained
> ¼ cup sliced scallions

1 In a vegetable steamer, cook the chicken until cooked through, 10 to 12 minutes. Transfer the chicken to a plate and set aside to cool. When cool enough to handle, cut the chicken into slices (reserve any juices that have collected on the plate).

2 In a small bowl, combine the lime zest, lime juice, honey, soy sauce, ginger, and any reserved chicken juices. Pour ⅓ cup of this dressing over the chicken slices and set aside to marinate in the refrigerator for at least 1 hour.

3 Line individual serving plates with shredded lettuce. Arrange the kiwi and water chestnut slices around the outside. Mound the chicken in the center and sprinkle with the scallions. Drizzle the remaining dressing over the salad (including any left in bowl the cooked chicken was marinating in). *Makes 4 servings*

Chicken Salad with Golden Kiwi & Jícama Substitute golden kiwifruit for the green. Omit the water chestnuts and use ½ cup of peeled and thinly sliced jícama. Substitute ¼ cup of diced red onion for the scallions.

Chicken Normandy

This healthy interpretation of a French regional dish uses apple juice concentrate to heighten the apple flavor and a small amount of fat-free half-and-half to give the sauce a creamy texture.

2 teaspoons olive oil
4 skinless, boneless chicken breast halves (5 ounces each)
1 large onion, halved and thinly sliced
3 Granny Smith apples, cut into ½-inch-thick wedges
3 tablespoons frozen apple juice concentrate
½ cup chicken broth, homemade (*page 32*) or
    reduced-sodium canned
½ teaspoon salt
½ teaspoon rubbed sage
3 tablespoons fat-free half-and-half

1 In a large nonstick skillet, heat the oil over medium-high heat. Add the chicken and cook until lightly browned on both sides, about 8 minutes. With a slotted spoon, transfer the chicken to a plate.

2 Add the onion to the skillet and cook, stirring frequently, until the onion is golden brown, about 7 minutes. Add the apple and apple juice concentrate, stirring to coat.

3 Add the broth and bring to a boil. Return the chicken to the pan. Sprinkle with the salt and sage and cook until the chicken is cooked through, about 5 minutes.

4 Transfer the chicken and apple wedges to serving plates. Whisk the half-and-half into the sauce in the pan and cook for 1 minute to heat through. Spoon the sauce over the chicken. ***Makes 4 servings***

Hawaiian Chicken Substitute canned pineapple chunks for the apples, and 3 tablespoons frozen pineapple juice concentrate for the apple juice concentrate. Add 2 tablespoons of ketchup when you add the broth in step 3. Omit the sage and the half-and-half.

turkey meatballs

Meatballs are a much over-looked option for including a little bit of meat in your diet without going overboard.

- Try serving any of these meatballs as an appetizer with a homemade dipping sauce (*see page 43*). The Asian Turkey Meatballs are particularly tasty with the Lemon-Herb Dipping Sauce.

- Add the meatballs to a store-bought marinara sauce for a quick pasta sauce.

- Add meatballs to a simple broth: Try Roasted Vegetable Broth (*page 32*).

- Add meatballs to a cream soup: Try "Cream" of Tomato Basil Soup (*page 27*).

Best of all, you can make several batches of these meatballs to have on hand. Form them into balls as directed in the recipe, then spread them out on a tray or large plate and freeze. When the meatballs are frozen hard, transfer them to a freezer container.

To cook the meatballs: Sauté them in a small amount of oil in a large nonstick skillet for about 10 minutes. Or broil them (on a broiler rack sprayed with nonstick spray) for about 7 minutes. Or, cook them in a simmering liquid (such as a soup or broth, see above) for about 5 minutes.

Asian Turkey Meatballs

10 ounces lean ground turkey

⅓ cup chopped cilantro

2 scallions, thinly sliced

2 cloves garlic, minced

2 tablespoons hoisin sauce or red currant jelly

1 large egg white

In a large bowl, stir together all of the ingredients. Shape into 24 walnut-size meatballs. ***Makes 24 meatballs***

PER MEATBALL: 24 CALORIES, 0.9G TOTAL FAT (0.3G SATURATED), 0MG CHOLESTEROL, 0G DIETARY FIBER, 1G CARBOHYDRATE, 3G PROTEIN, 38MG SODIUM

Basil-Tomato Turkey Meatballs

¼ cup sun-dried tomatoes (not oil-packed)

½ cup boiling water

10 ounces lean ground turkey

1 large egg white

⅓ cup chopped fresh basil

2 tablespoons plain dried breadcrumbs

2 tablespoons grated Parmesan cheese

1 In a medium heatproof bowl, combine the sun-dried tomatoes and boiling water. Let stand until the tomatoes have softened, 15 to 20 minutes (depending on the dryness of the tomatoes). Drain,

reserving 2 tablespoons of the soaking liquid, and finely chop the tomatoes.

2 In a large bowl, stir together the chopped sun-dried tomatoes, reserved tomato soaking liquid, turkey, egg white, basil, breadcrumbs, and Parmesan. Shape into 24 walnut-size meatballs. ***Makes 24 meatballs***

PER MEATBALL: 24 CALORIES, 1.1G TOTAL FAT (0.4G SATURATED), 0MG CHOLESTEROL, 0G DIETARY FIBER, 1G CARBOHYDRATE, 3G PROTEIN, 38MG SODIUM

Scallion-Mustard Turkey Meatballs

10 ounces lean ground turkey

1 large egg white

1 apple (6 ounces), unpeeled, grated

2 scallions, thinly sliced

2 cloves garlic, minced

2 tablespoons old-fashioned rolled oats

2 teaspoons Dijon mustard

In a large bowl, stir together all the ingredients. Shape into 24 walnut-size meatballs. ***Makes 24 meatballs***

PER MEATBALL: 25 CALORIES, 0.9G TOTAL FAT (0.3G SATURATED), 0MG CHOLESTEROL, 0G DIETARY FIBER, 2G CARBOHYDRATE, 3G PROTEIN, 22MG SODIUM

Chicken Stew with Peas & Mushrooms

Serve this stew on a bed of wide yolkless egg noodles or over mashed potatoes.

per serving	
calories	238
total fat	6.3g
saturated fat	1.4g
cholesterol	74mg
dietary fiber	3g
carbohydrate	13g
protein	23g
sodium	447mg

good source of: niacin, selenium

2 teaspoons olive oil
2 tablespoons diced Canadian bacon
1 medium red onion, finely chopped
1 teaspoon sugar
1 cup dry red wine
¾ cup chicken broth, homemade (*page 32*) or reduced-sodium canned
½ teaspoon tarragon
¼ teaspoon salt
¾ pound skinless, boneless chicken thigh, cut into 1-inch chunks
½ pound small mushrooms, quartered
1 cup frozen peas, thawed
2 teaspoons cornstarch blended with 1 tablespoon water

1 In a large nonstick skillet, heat the oil over medium heat. Add the Canadian bacon and cook 1 minute. Add the onion and sprinkle with the sugar. Cook until the onion begins to brown, about 7 minutes.

2 Add the wine, bring to a boil, and boil for 2 minutes. Add the broth, tarragon, and salt, and return to a boil. Add the chicken and mushrooms. Cover, reduce to a simmer, and cook until the chicken is cooked through, 4 to 5 minutes.

3 Stir in the peas and the cornstarch mixture, and cook until the peas are heated through and the sauce is slightly thickened, about 1 minute. ***Makes 4 servings***

Pineapple-Broiled Chicken & Apple Salad

per serving	
calories	271
total fat	5.3g
saturated fat	1.2g
cholesterol	63mg
dietary fiber	4g
carbohydrate	31g
protein	26g
sodium	641mg

good source of: folate, niacin, potassium, selenium, vitamin B$_6$, vitamin C

If it works for your schedule, the chicken can marinate for as long as overnight in this sweet and spicy marinade

> Pineapple-Ginger Marinade (*page 56*)
> 4 small skinless, boneless chicken breast halves (4 ounces each)
> 2 Granny Smith apples, unpeeled, cut into ½-inch-wide wedges
> 2 celery stalks, cut into matchsticks
> 1 small red onion, halved and thinly sliced
> 8 cups shredded romaine lettuce

1 In a large bowl, make the Pineapple-Ginger Marinade. Measure out ½ cup of the mixture to use as a marinade for the chicken, and place in a large zip-seal plastic bag. Set aside the remainder to use as a salad dressing in step 3.

2 Add the chicken to the marinade in the zip-seal bag and seal. Refrigerate 1 to 2 hours, turning the bag once or twice.

3 Preheat the broiler. Spray the broiler pan with nonstick cooking spray. Lift the chicken from the marinade, reserving any marinade in the bag. Broil the chicken 4 to 6 inches from the heat for 2 minutes. Brush with half of the marinade and broil 2 minutes longer. Turn the chicken over, brush with the remaining marinade, and broil until the chicken is cooked through, about 4 minutes.

4 Meanwhile, to the bowl with the reserved pineapple-ginger mixture, add the apple wedges, celery, onion, and lettuce, and toss to coat.

5 Place the lettuce mixture on 4 plates. Slice each chicken breast on the diagonal and place on top of the salad. *Makes 4 servings*

Broiled Chicken & Rice Salad Prepare 1½ times the recipe for Pineapple-Ginger Marinade. Measure out ½ cup to be used to marinate and baste the chicken (the remainder goes into the bowl with the apples, as described in step 4). Add 2 cups of cooked brown rice and 3 tablespoons coarsely chopped pecans to the bowl with the apples, celery, and onion, but omit the lettuce. Toss to combine. Slice the chicken and serve on top of the salad.

Chicken Chow Mein

Chow mein is traditionally served over fried noodles, but our version uses whole-wheat spaghetti instead, saving on fat and calories as well as adding some extra fiber. If you prefer, substitute wide, flat noodles for the spaghetti.

per serving	
calories	349
total fat	6.6g
saturated fat	1.1g
cholesterol	49mg
dietary fiber	7g
carbohydrate	45g
protein	29g
sodium	592mg

good source of: beta carotene, niacin, selenium, vitamin B$_6$, vitamin C

8 ounces whole-wheat spaghetti
1 cup chicken broth, homemade (*page 32*) or
    reduced-sodium canned
3 tablespoons reduced-sodium soy sauce
1 tablespoon sherry or apple juice
2 teaspoons dark sesame oil
1½ teaspoons cornstarch
2 teaspoons olive oil
1 large red bell pepper, slivered
6 cups packaged coleslaw mixture
¾ pound skinless, boneless chicken breasts, cut across
    the grain into ½-inch-wide strips
4 scallions, cut into 2-inch lengths

KITCHEN *tip*

Packaged coleslaw mixture, a combination of shredded green cabbage and carrots, is available in bags in the produce section of most supermarkets.

1 In a large pot of boiling water, cook the pasta according to package directions. Drain.

2 Meanwhile, in a small bowl, whisk the broth, soy sauce, sherry, and sesame oil into the cornstarch.

3 In a large nonstick skillet or wok, heat the olive oil over medium-high heat. Add the bell pepper and coleslaw mixture, and cook, stirring frequently, until the pepper is crisp-tender, about 3 minutes.

4 Add the chicken and stir-fry until the chicken is cooked through, about 4 minutes.

5 Add the drained pasta and scallions, stirring to coat. Stir the broth mixture to recombine and add it to the pan. Cook, stirring, until the pasta is coated and heated through, about 2 minutes. ***Makes 4 servings***

F.Y.I.

Dried plums (most of us still call them "prunes") furnish more than their well-known laxative benefits. Along with magnesium, iron, and potassium, dried plums provide good amounts of fiber—both soluble and insoluble. And recent research has shed light on the antioxidant potential of dried plums. In fact, in one well-known study they appear at the top of a long list of fruits and vegetables tested for antioxidant status. In addition, experimental studies indicate that dried plums may help to lower LDL cholesterol, making them a potential boon for heart health.

Chicken with Red Wine & Dried Plums

Dried plums (a.k.a. prunes) not only provide fiber and flavor, but they give body and richness to the finished sauce. If you can't find bite-size dried plums, cut large dried plums into bite-size pieces.

2 teaspoons olive oil
1½ cups sliced carrots
8 scallions, cut into 2-inch lengths
1⅓ cups dry red wine
1¼ cups bite-size pitted dried plums (prunes)
½ teaspoon salt
½ teaspoon pepper
1 pound skinless, boneless chicken thighs, cut into
   1-inch chunks

1 In a large nonstick skillet, heat the oil over medium heat. Add the carrots, and cook until they are crisp-tender, about 5 minutes. Add the scallions, stirring to coat.

2 Add the wine, dried plums, salt, and pepper, and bring to a boil. Reduce to a simmer, add the chicken, cover, and cook until the chicken is cooked through and the plums are tender, about 10 minutes.

3 With the back of a spoon, mash about one-fourth of the plums to give some thickness to the sauce. ***Makes 4 servings***

Country Captain

A classic curry recipe from the American south, Country Captain is said to have been named for a British officer who brought it to this country after a stay in India.

On the Menu

Traditionally, Country Captain is served with rice, but try steamed shredded cabbage with caraway seeds to serve with this fragrant curry. Serve a crusty whole-wheat peasant bread on the side. For dessert, offer Indian-inspired Baked Spiced Carrot Pudding (*page 126*).

⅔ cup rice
¾ teaspoon salt
2 teaspoons olive oil
4 small skinless, boneless chicken breast halves
   (4 ounces each)
2 tablespoons flour
1 tablespoon curry powder
¾ teaspoon thyme
2 medium onions, chopped
2 large green bell peppers, diced
3 cloves garlic, minced
¼ cup water
1 can (14½ ounces) no-salt-added tomatoes, chopped
   with their juice
1 can (8 ounces) no-salt-added tomato sauce
½ cup raisins
2 tablespoons sliced almonds

1 In a medium saucepan, cook the rice according to package directions, using ¼ teaspoon of the salt.

2 Meanwhile, in a large nonstick skillet, heat the oil over medium heat. Dust the chicken with the flour, shaking off the excess. Add the chicken to the pan and sauté until golden brown on both sides, about 5 minutes. Transfer the chicken to a plate.

3 Add the curry powder and thyme to the skillet and cook for 30 seconds. Add the onions, bell peppers, and garlic, and stir to coat. Add the water and cook, stirring frequently, until the vegetables are softened, about 5 minutes.

4 Stir in the tomatoes, tomato sauce, raisins, and remaining ½ teaspoon salt, and bring to a boil. Reduce to a simmer and cook 4 minutes. Return the chicken to the pan, cover, and cook until the chicken is cooked through and the vegetables are tender, about 10 minutes. Stir in the almonds. Serve the chicken mixture over the rice. ***Makes 4 servings***

Stir-Fried Red Vegetables & Chicken

The technique of stir-frying preserves the colors, flavors, and textures of all the ingredients in the dish. In this unusual stir-fry, three red vegetables (onion, cabbage, and bell pepper) are combined with strips of chicken in a hot-and-sweet sauce.

per serving	
calories	264
total fat	8.4g
saturated fat	1.3g
cholesterol	66mg
dietary fiber	3g
carbohydrate	16g
protein	28g
sodium	83mg

good source of: niacin, selenium, vitamin B$_6$, vitamin C

1 tablespoon cornstarch
⅓ cup dry sherry
2 tablespoons reduced-sodium soy sauce
1 tablespoon minced garlic
1 tablespoon light brown sugar
½ teaspoon crushed red pepper flakes
2 tablespoons olive oil
1 pound skinless, boneless chicken breast, cut across the
    grain into ½-inch-wide strips
1 large red onion, halved and thickly sliced
1½ cups finely shredded red cabbage
2 medium red bell peppers, cut into strips

1 In a small cup or bowl, blend the cornstarch with the sherry, soy sauce, garlic, brown sugar, and red pepper flakes. Set aside.

2 In a large nonstick skillet, heat 2 teaspoons of oil the over medium-high heat. Add the chicken and stir-fry until just barely cooked, about 2 minutes. With a slotted spoon, transfer the chicken to a plate.

3 Add 2 teaspoons of the oil to the skillet and heat. Add the onion and stir-fry until softened, about 3 minutes. Add the remaining 2 teaspoons oil, cabbage, and bell peppers, and stir-fry until the peppers are crisp-tender, about 2 minutes.

4 Add the reserved sherry-soy sauce mixture to the skillet along with the chicken (and any juices that have collected on the plate). Cook over medium-high heat until the sauce thickens and the chicken is cooked through, about 3 minutes. ***Makes 4 servings***

Chicken & Shiitake Mushrooms en Papillote

The foil packets can be assembled up to 8 hours in advance and refrigerated. At serving time, pop them in the oven and bake for a quick yet elegant dinner. Allow a few more minutes of cooking time if the packets come straight from the refrigerator.

per serving	
calories	241
total fat	7g
saturated fat	1.7g
cholesterol	94mg
dietary fiber	1g
carbohydrate	6g
protein	36g
sodium	469mg

good source of:
niacin, selenium, vitamin B₆, vitamin C

2 teaspoons olive oil
2 slices (1 ounce) turkey bacon, coarsely chopped
½ pound shiitake mushrooms, stems discarded and caps finely chopped
3 cloves garlic, minced
1 small red bell pepper, finely chopped
½ teaspoon thyme
½ teaspoon salt
½ teaspoon black pepper
4 small skinless, boneless chicken breast halves (4 ounces each)
1 tablespoon fresh lemon juice

1 Preheat the oven to 425°F.

2 In a large nonstick skillet, heat the oil over medium heat. Add the bacon and cook until lightly browned around the edges, about 4 minutes. Add the mushrooms and garlic and cook until the mushrooms are soft, about 5 minutes. Add the bell pepper, thyme, salt, and black pepper, and cook until the bell pepper is tender, about 4 minutes. Remove from the heat.

3 Cut four pieces of foil 12 x 18 inches each. With a short end of the foil facing you, place 1 chicken breast half on the bottom half of each sheet. Sprinkle with the lemon juice and spoon the mushroom mixture on top.

4 Fold the foil over the chicken, folding the edges over to seal. Place the packets on a baking sheet and bake 12 to 15 minutes, or until the chicken is cooked through. Carefully open one packet (be careful—steam will escape) and check for doneness. If the chicken isn't done, reseal the packet and return the baking sheet to the oven. ***Makes 4 servings***

KITCHEN tip

Although turkey bacon tastes a lot like regular bacon, and even looks a bit like it, it has no fat to speak of. So to cook turkey bacon, you need to start with a little bit of oil in the pan so the bacon won't stick. The object is to cook the bacon until it's lightly browned around the edges, caramelizing it a bit to bring out its flavor. But turkey bacon will never get really crisp the way regular bacon does.

Turkey, Chick-Pea & Corn Chili

This chili is a powerhouse of nutrients, with outstanding amounts of beta carotene, B vitamins (including heart-healthy folate), fiber, and potassium.

per serving	
calories	448
total fat	6g
saturated fat	0.9g
cholesterol	70mg
dietary fiber	12g
carbohydrate	62g
protein	40g
sodium	891mg

good source of: beta carotene, fiber, folate, magnesium, niacin, potassium, riboflavin, selenium, thiamin, vitamin B$_6$, vitamin C, vitamin E, zinc

2 teaspoons olive oil
1 large onion, chopped
3 cloves garlic, slivered
1 pound sweet potatoes, peeled and cut into ½-inch chunks
1 tablespoon chili powder
¾ teaspoon salt
1 cup water
1¾ cups canned crushed tomatoes
1 can (19 ounces) chick-peas, rinsed and drained
1 pound skinless, boneless turkey breast, cut into ½-inch chunks
1½ cups frozen corn kernels, thawed

1 In a nonstick Dutch oven, heat the oil over medium heat. Add the onion and garlic, and cook, stirring frequently, until the onion is tender, about 5 minutes.

2 Add the sweet potatoes, chili powder, and salt, stirring to coat. Add the water and bring to a boil. Cover and gently boil until the sweet potatoes are almost tender, about 5 minutes.

3 Add the tomatoes, chick-peas, and turkey. Reduce the heat to a simmer, cover, and cook until the turkey is cooked through, about 5 minutes. Add the corn and cook until heated through, about 2 minutes. ***Makes 4 servings***

Moroccan Turkey & Chick-Pea Stew Omit the chili powder and use 1½ teaspoons ground coriander, 1 teaspoon paprika, and ½ teaspoon ground cumin instead (add in step 2). Omit the corn. Just before serving, stir in ⅓ cup chopped cilantro.

Spotlite recipe

Extra-Moist Turkey Loaf

1 cup carrot juice
1 large onion, finely chopped
3 cloves garlic, minced
1 pound skinless, boneless turkey breast, cut into large chunks
½ cup quick-cooking oats
¼ cup prune butter
1 tablespoon Dijon mustard
1 large egg white
¾ teaspoon salt
½ teaspoon rubbed sage

1 Preheat the oven to 350°F. In a small skillet, combine ½ cup of the carrot juice, the onion, and garlic, and cook over low heat until the onion is tender and the liquid has been absorbed, about 10 minutes. Transfer the onion mixture to a large bowl and let cool to room temperature. Stir in the remaining ½ cup carrot juice.

2 In a food processor, pulse the turkey until finely ground.

3 Add the turkey to the bowl with the onion mixture and stir to combine. Stir in the oats, prune butter, mustard, egg white, salt, and sage.

4 Spoon the mixture into an 8½ x 4½-inch loaf pan. Bake 50 minutes, or until the turkey is cooked through. Cool 10 minutes in the pan, then run a spatula around the edges and invert the turkey loaf onto a serving platter. *Makes 4 servings*

PER SERVING **256 calories, 1.9g total fat (0.4g saturated), 70mg cholesterol, 3g dietary fiber, 27g carbohydrate, 32g protein, 619mg sodium**
Good source of: **beta carotene, niacin, selenium, vitamin B₆**

Prune butter may be best known for its role in low-fat baking. Lots of low-fat recipes—especially for brownies—call for prune butter to replace some of the fat. However, it can also play a role in savory dishes. Prune butter is used in this recipe to provide moisture and a hint of sweetness, as well as some fiber. The other ingredients that contribute to the exceptionally moist texture of this turkey loaf are carrot juice (with a handsome amount of beta carotene) and heart-healthy oats.

Spaghetti with Chicken Meatballs

Chicken thigh meat makes exceptionally flavorful and moist meatballs. When you form meatballs from ground poultry, it's a good idea to moisten your hands to keep the meatball mixture from sticking.

per serving	
calories	598
total fat	12g
saturated fat	3.5g
cholesterol	81mg
dietary fiber	6g
carbohydrate	81g
protein	38g
sodium	540mg

good source of: niacin, riboflavin, selenium, vitamin C, zinc

On the *Menu*

Start off the meal with sliced oranges and chopped watercress sprinkled with black pepper and balsamic vinegar. For dessert, offer Fresh Grape Gelatin (*page 131*).

¾ pound skinless, boneless chicken thighs, cut into chunks
½ cup minced scallions
1 clove garlic, minced
¼ teaspoon rubbed sage
¼ cup fat-free milk
3 tablespoons grated Parmesan cheese
3 tablespoons plain dried breadcrumbs
½ teaspoon salt
1 large egg white
2 cans (14½ ounces each) no-salt-added stewed tomatoes, coarsely chopped with their juice
2 teaspoons paprika
¼ teaspoon cayenne pepper
12 ounces spaghetti

1 In a food processor, finely grind the chicken. Add the scallions, garlic, and sage, and process until combined. Add the milk, Parmesan, breadcrumbs, salt, and egg white. Process to combine. Form the mixture into 24 meatballs.

2 In a large nonstick skillet, stir together the tomatoes, paprika, and cayenne. Bring to a boil and cook 4 minutes, then reduce to a simmer. Add the meatballs, cover, and cook 10 minutes, or until the meatballs are cooked through and the sauce is flavorful.

3 Meanwhile, in a large pot of boiling water, cook the pasta according to package directions. Drain. Spoon the meatballs and sauce over the pasta. *Makes 4 servings*

Spaghetti & Basil-Tomato Meatballs Skip step 1 and make the Basil-Tomato Turkey Meatballs (*page 70*).

Stir-Fried Chicken & Tofu

per serving	
calories	336
total fat	16g
saturated fat	2.5g
cholesterol	50mg
dietary fiber	2g
carbohydrate	16g
protein	34g
sodium	605mg

good source of: magnesium, niacin, selenium, vitamin B$_6$, vitamin C

Instead of the more obvious choice of rice, serve this stir-fry over barley. The barley contributes a significant amount of fiber (about 25% of which is heart-healthy soluble fiber), as well as lots of the antioxidant mineral selenium and quite a bit of magnesium.

¼ cup reduced-sodium soy sauce
1 tablespoon light brown sugar
2 teaspoons cornstarch
¾ pound skinless, boneless chicken breasts, cut crosswise
    into ¼-inch-wide strips
2 tablespoons olive oil
½ pound shiitake mushrooms, stems discarded and caps
    quartered
1 red bell pepper, cut into ½-inch squares
½ pound asparagus, cut on the diagonal into 1-inch
    lengths
2 cloves garlic, minced
1 tablespoon minced fresh ginger
1 pound extra-firm tofu, cut into ½-inch chunks
4 scallions, thinly sliced

1 In a medium bowl, whisk together the soy sauce, brown sugar, and corn-starch. Add the chicken and stir to coat.

2 In a large nonstick skillet, heat the oil over medium-high heat. Add the mushrooms and bell pepper, and cook, stirring frequently, until the pepper is crisp-tender, about 3 minutes.

3 Lift the chicken from the marinade, reserving the marinade. Add the chicken to the pan along with the asparagus, garlic, and ginger and cook, stirring, until the chicken is almost cooked through, about 3 minutes.

4 Add the tofu, scallions, and reserved marinade, and bring to a boil. Cook, stirring frequently, until the chicken is cooked through and the sauce is slightly thickened, about 3 minutes. ***Makes 4 servings***

per serving	
calories	460
total fat	7.6g
saturated fat	4g
cholesterol	72mg
dietary fiber	7g
carbohydrate	76g
protein	21g
sodium	574mg

good source of: beta carotene, folate, niacin, potassium, riboflavin, selenium, thiamin, vitamin B$_6$, vitamin C

KITCHEN *tip*

If you don't have a 2-inch cookie cutter, you can cut out the dumplings using a small, thin-rimmed glass, such as a wineglass.

Baked Potato-Mozzarella Dumplings

Though most dumplings are cooked soup or broth, these potato dumplings (which are somewhat like Italian gnocchi) are topped with Parmesan and baked instead. The tomato sauce can be made well in advance.

2 large carrots, thinly sliced
1 large baking potato (8 ounces), peeled and thinly sliced
1 cup water
3 cloves garlic, slivered
½ teaspoon salt
1 small red bell pepper, minced
1 large egg
2 large egg whites
1 cup shredded part-skim mozzarella cheese
2 cups flour
2 tablespoons grated Parmesan cheese
1 can (14½ ounces) Italian-style diced tomatoes
1 can (8 ounces) no-salt-added tomato sauce
2 tablespoons chopped fresh basil

1 In a large saucepan, combine the carrots, potato, water, garlic, and ¼ teaspoon of the salt. Bring to a boil over medium heat. Reduce to a simmer, cover, and cook until the vegetables are soft, about 12 minutes. Drain any liquid. Press the mixture through a sieve set over a bowl. Set aside to cool.

2 Preheat the oven to 425°F. Spray a baking sheet with nonstick cooking spray.

3 Add the remaining ¼ teaspoon salt, the bell pepper, whole egg, egg whites, and mozzarella to the mashed vegetables and blend well. Stir in the flour until the mixture forms a dough stiff enough to pat out.

4 On a lightly floured board, pat the dough out to a 9-inch round about ½ inch thick. With a 2-inch round cutter, cut the dough into rounds and place in a single layer on the baking sheet. Gather the scraps, re-roll, and cut for a total of 24. Sprinkle with the Parmesan and bake for 20 minutes, or until golden.

5 Meanwhile, in a large nonstick skillet, combine the diced tomatoes and tomato sauce. Bring to a boil, reduce to a simmer, and cook until slightly thickened, about 5 minutes. Stir in the basil and spoon the sauce over the dumplings. *Makes 4 servings*

Recipes for a Healthy Heart

Shiitake Mushroom Burgers

These faux "burgers" are made with fresh shiitake mushrooms (plus some dried, for a flavor boost), bulgur, and some shredded mozzarella to help hold things together.

½ cup dried shiitake mushrooms (½ ounce)
1 cup boiling water
3 slices (1 ounce each) firm sandwich bread
1 pound fresh shiitake mushrooms, stems discarded and
    caps quartered
3 teaspoons olive oil
1 small onion, finely chopped
1 carrot, finely chopped
3 cloves garlic, minced
⅔ cup bulgur
¾ teaspoon salt
½ teaspoon rosemary, minced
3 ounces part-skim mozzarella cheese, shredded

ON THE *Menu*

Though they are called burgers and thus suggest the use of hamburger buns, these mushroom patties are delicious on toasted whole-grain bread with a skim of mustard, thinly sliced red onions, and lots of oak leaf lettuce.

1 In a small heatproof bowl, combine the dried mushrooms and the boiling water, and let stand for 20 minutes or until softened. Reserving the soaking liquid, scoop out the dried mushrooms and finely chop. Strain the soaking liquid through a coffee filter or a paper towel-lined sieve.

2 In a food processor, process the bread until finely crumbed. Set the breadcrumbs aside. Add the fresh mushrooms to the processor and process until finely chopped.

3 In a large nonstick saucepan, heat 2 teaspoons of the oil over low heat. Add the onion, carrot, and garlic, and cook, stirring frequently, until the onion is tender, about 7 minutes. Add the fresh mushrooms and reconstituted dried mushrooms, and stir to combine.

4 Add the bulgur, salt, rosemary, and mushroom soaking liquid. Increase the heat to medium, cover, and cook, stirring occasionally, for 10 minutes. Uncover and cook until the bulgur is tender and the liquid has been absorbed, 5 to 7 minutes.

5 Transfer the bulgur mixture to a large bowl. Let cool to room temperature. Stir in the breadcrumbs and mozzarella.

6 In a large nonstick skillet, heat the remaining 1 teaspoon oil over medium heat. Shape the mushroom mixture into 4 patties. Cook until crusty and heated through, about 3 minutes per side. ***Makes 4 servings***

Baked Fusilli with Mushrooms

You can use all cremini mushrooms, or all button mushrooms. The broccoli can be replaced with small cauliflower florets.

10 ounces whole-wheat short fusilli
¼ cup water
6 cloves garlic, minced
1 pound button mushrooms, thinly sliced
½ pound cremini mushrooms, thinly sliced
4 cups broccoli florets
2½ cups low-fat (1%) milk
3 tablespoons flour
¾ teaspoon salt
¼ teaspoon pepper
⅓ cup grated Parmesan cheese

1 Preheat the oven to 425°F. Spray a 9 x 13-inch baking dish with nonstick cooking spray. In a large pot of boiling water, cook the fusilli according to package directions. Drain.

2 Meanwhile, in a Dutch oven or flameproof casserole, bring the water and garlic to a boil over medium heat. Add the mushrooms and broccoli, and cook, stirring occasionally, until the broccoli is tender, about 5 minutes.

3 In a medium bowl, whisk the milk into the flour until smooth. Stir the milk mixture into the pan with the mushrooms and broccoli. Add the salt and pepper, and cook, stirring frequently, until the mixture is slightly thickened, about 2 minutes. Add the drained fusilli and the Parmesan, and stir to combine.

4 Spoon the pasta mixture into the baking dish and bake for 15 minutes, or until the top is light golden. *Makes 6 servings*

KITCHEN tip

Although most cookbooks tell you to avoid button mushrooms with exposed gills (the dark part underneath the cap), these slightly "older" mushrooms actually have more flavor.

Off-the-Shelf

If you happen to have all of these ingredients on your pantry shelf (or in the freezer), you can have a simple, nutritious dinner on the table in under an hour. All you might want to round out the meal is a tossed green salad.

Spicy Tortilla-Vegetable Casserole

2 packages (12 ounces each) frozen winter squash
   puree, thawed
1 tablespoon sugar
¼ teaspoon salt
1 can (15½ ounces) red kidney beans, rinsed and
   drained
1 package (8 ounces) cut-up frozen asparagus, thawed
1 cup frozen corn kernels, thawed
½ cup mild to medium bottled salsa
36 low-fat baked tortilla chips (2 ounces)
½ cup shredded reduced-fat Cheddar cheese

1 Preheat the oven to 375°F. Spray a 9-inch square glass baking dish with nonstick cooking spray. In a medium bowl, combine the squash, sugar, and salt.

2 Stir in the beans, asparagus, corn, and salsa. Spoon half of the squash-vegetable mixture into the baking dish. Top with the tortilla chips (spread them evenly) and then the remaining squash-vegetable mixture.

3 Cover with foil and bake for 25 minutes. Uncover, sprinkle the Cheddar over the top, and bake until the filling is piping hot and the cheese has melted, about 5 minutes. ***Makes 4 servings***

PER SERVING 335 calories, 3.5g total fat (1.3g saturated), 6mg cholesterol, 11g dietary fiber, 67g carbohydrate, 17g protein, 594mg sodium
Good source of: beta carotene, fiber, folate, potassium, thiamin, vitamin B$_6$, vitamin C

Vegetarian Chili

Sweet potatoes vary in dryness depending upon their age and type, so in step 5, check the potatoes after 10 minutes. If they seem to be almost tender, don't cook for the full 20 minutes; just skip to the part where you add the corn—the final 5 minutes of cooking will ensure that the sweet potatoes are tender.

per serving	
calories	453
total fat	5.5g
saturated fat	0.8g
cholesterol	0mg
dietary fiber	19g
carbohydrate	88g
protein	21g
sodium	837mg

good source of: beta carotene, fiber, folate, magnesium, niacin, potassium, riboflavin, thiamin, vitamin B_6, vitamin C, vitamin E, zinc

F.Y.I.

The corn, spinach, and tomatoes in this vegetarian chili all provide lutein, a natural plant pigment linked with eye health.

 1 cup dried red kidney beans (8 ounces), rinsed
　　and picked over
 1 tablespoon olive oil
 1 medium red onion, chopped
 2 cloves garlic, minced
 1 green bell pepper, cut into ½-inch squares
 1 pound sweet potatoes, peeled and cut into 1-inch
　　chunks
 2 teaspoons chili powder
 1 teaspoon salt
 ¾ teaspoon cinnamon
 ¾ teaspoon coriander
 2 cans (8 ounces each) no-salt-added tomato sauce
 1 package (10 ounces) frozen chopped spinach, thawed
　　and drained
 1 package (10 ounces) frozen corn kernels, thawed

1　In a medium saucepan, combine the beans and cold water to cover by 2 inches. Bring to a boil and boil 2 minutes. Let stand 1 hour. Drain.

2　Return the drained beans to the saucepan. Add cold water to cover by 2 inches and bring to a boil. Reduce to a simmer, partially cover, and cook until the beans are tender, about 1 hour. Drain, reserving ½ cup of the bean cooking liquid.

3　Meanwhile, in a Dutch oven or flameproof casserole, heat the oil over medium-low heat. Add the onion and garlic, and cook, stirring frequently, until the onion is tender, about 7 minutes. Add the bell pepper and cook, stirring frequently, until tender, about 5 minutes.

4　Stir in the sweet potatoes, chili powder, salt, cinnamon, and coriander until coated. Add the tomato sauce and 1 cup of water and bring to a boil. Reduce to a simmer, cover, and cook 20 minutes.

5　Stir in the spinach, beans, and reserved bean cooking liquid. Return to a boil, reduce to a simmer, cover, and until the sweet potatoes are tender, about 20 minutes. Add the corn and cook for 5 minutes to heat through.
Makes 4 servings

Bean & Potato Salad with Mozzarella

per serving	
calories	308
total fat	4.5g
saturated fat	0.6g
cholesterol	10mg
dietary fiber	8g
carbohydrate	43g
protein	25g
sodium	845mg

good source of: calcium, fiber, folate, potassium, vitamin B$_6$, vitamin C

If you like spicy food, use spicy tomato-vegetable juice in the tomato-mustard salad dressing.

³⁄₄ pound small red potatoes, quartered
³⁄₄ cup tomato-vegetable juice
2 tablespoons red wine vinegar
1 tablespoon Dijon mustard
1 tablespoon olive oil
¹⁄₃ cup chopped fresh basil
¹⁄₂ teaspoon black pepper
2 cups cherry tomatoes, halved
1 yellow bell pepper, cut into ¹⁄₂-inch squares
1 red onion, halved and thinly sliced
1 can (15 ounces) red kidney beans, rinsed and drained
8 ounces fat-free mozzarella cheese, cut into ¹⁄₂-inch cubes

1 In a large pot of boiling water, cook the potatoes until tender, about 10 minutes. Drain well.

2 Meanwhile, in a large bowl, whisk together the tomato-vegetable juice, vinegar, mustard, oil, basil, and black pepper.

3 Add the potatoes to the dressing and toss to coat. Add the tomatoes, bell pepper, onion, beans, and mozzarella, and toss again. Serve at room temperature or chilled. *Makes 4 servings*

Dilled White Bean & Potato Salad Use cannellini beans instead of red kidney beans and minced fresh dill instead of basil. Substitute white wine vinegar for the red.

Spotlite recipe

Quinoa with Fennel, Raisins & Parmesan

⅓ cup sun-dried tomatoes (not oil-packed)
1 cup boiling water
1 tablespoon olive oil
1 fennel bulb (12 ounces), trimmed and cut into ½-inch chunks
3 cloves garlic, minced
1⅔ cups quinoa, rinsed and well drained
1 teaspoon fennel seeds, crushed
1 teaspoon salt
½ cup golden raisins
¼ cup grated Parmesan cheese

1　In a small heatproof bowl, combine the sun-dried tomatoes and boiling water. Let stand until the tomatoes have softened, 15 to 20 minutes (depending on the dryness of the tomatoes). Drain, reserving the soaking liquid, and coarsely chop the tomatoes.

2　In a nonstick Dutch oven, heat the oil over medium heat. Add the fresh fennel and garlic, and cook, stirring frequently, until the fennel is tender, about 7 minutes.

3　Stir in the quinoa, fennel seeds, and salt, and cook, stirring frequently, until the quinoa is dry, about 5 minutes.

4　Add the reserved tomato soaking liquid and 1½ cups of water, and bring to a boil. Reduce to a simmer, cover, and cook, until the quinoa is tender, 12 to 15 minutes.

5　Stir in the chopped sun-dried tomatoes, raisins, and Parmesan. *Makes 4 servings*

PER SERVING **419 calories, 9.8g total fat (2.1g saturated), 5mg cholesterol, 8g dietary fiber, 73g carbohydrate, 14g protein, 840mg sodium**
Good source of: **fiber, magnesium, potassium, riboflavin, vitamin E, zinc**

Tofu & Red Pepper Stir-Fry

per serving	
calories	122
total fat	4g
saturated fat	0.6g
cholesterol	0mg
dietary fiber	4g
carbohydrate	15g
protein	8g
sodium	558mg

good source of: beta carotene, vitamin C

For an interesting change of pace—and an extra measure of soluble fiber—serve the vegetables and tofu over bulgur instead of rice.

1 tablespoon olive oil
2 red bell peppers, cut into 1-inch squares
3 cloves garlic, minced
1 tablespoon minced fresh ginger
1 teaspoon sugar
3 tablespoons rice vinegar
½ pound sugar snap peas, strings removed
8 ounces extra-firm tofu, cut into ½-inch chunks
3 tablespoons reduced-sodium soy sauce
½ teaspoon cornstarch
¼ teaspoon salt
3 tablespoons water

1 In a large nonstick skillet or wok, heat the oil over medium heat. Add the bell peppers, garlic, and ginger. Sprinkle the sugar and 1 tablespoon of the vinegar over the vegetables and stir-fry until the peppers are crisp-tender, about 3 minutes.

2 Add the sugar snaps and stir-fry until crisp-tender, about 2 minutes. Add the tofu and stir very gently until just heated through, about 2 minutes.

3 In a small bowl, stir the remaining 2 tablespoons vinegar and the soy sauce into the cornstarch. Add the salt and water, whisk again, and pour the mixture over the vegetables. Cook, stirring gently, until the sauce is slightly thickened, about 1 minute. *Makes 4 servings*

Thai Noodles with Tofu

The mixture of sweet, tart, and savory is typical of many Southeast Asian cuisines. If you're making this dish in the summer, you can serve it at room temperature or chilled. For a dish with a bit more heft (but not a lot more calories), add ½ pound of cooked, shelled shrimp.

8 ounces linguine
⅓ cup ketchup
3 tablespoons reduced-sodium soy sauce
3 tablespoons fresh lime juice
1 tablespoon creamy peanut butter
2 teaspoons honey
¼ teaspoon salt
¼ cup chopped cilantro
2 scallions, thinly sliced
2 carrots, shredded
2 red bell peppers, cut into thin slivers
8 ounces low-fat extra-firm silken tofu, cut into ½-inch
  chunks

1 In a large pot of boiling water, cook the linguine according to package directions. Drain.

2 Meanwhile, in a large bowl, whisk together the ketchup, soy sauce, lime juice, peanut butter, honey, and salt. Whisk in the cilantro and scallions. Add the warm linguine and toss to coat.

3 Add the carrots and bell peppers to the bowl and toss to combine. Add the tofu and gently toss. ***Makes 4 servings***

per serving	
calories	337
total fat	3.7g
saturated fat	0.7g
cholesterol	0mg
dietary fiber	5g
carbohydrate	64g
protein	15g
sodium	880mg

good source of:
beta carotene, selenium, vitamin C

F.Y.I.

While soy protein is a heart-healthy component of soy foods, the protein content of tofu varies by brand or type. Firmer types of tofu have more protein whereas softer varieties contain more water, and as a result, offer less protein.

Mac & Cheese

In this healthful version of a comfort food favorite, cauliflower is added to give the impression of more pasta, but with fewer calories. Cauliflower also happens to be a good source of the heart-healthy B vitamin folate, as well as phytochemicals that may have cancer-fighting potential.

8 ounces elbow macaroni
2½ cups low-fat (1%) milk
3 tablespoons yellow cornmeal
1 tablespoon Dijon mustard
2 teaspoons chili powder
¾ teaspoon salt
3 cups frozen cauliflower, thawed
1 red bell pepper, diced
1½ cups fat-free cottage cheese
⅓ cup grated Parmesan cheese

ON THE *Menu*

Serve this simple baked pasta dish with a chopped salad of cherry tomatoes, scallions, and romaine lettuce tossed with a fat-free honey-mustard dressing. For dessert, serve Baked Apples with Date-Nut Stuffing (*page 122*).

1 Preheat the oven to 400°F. In a large pot of boiling water, cook the pasta according to package directions. Drain, reserving ¼ cup of the pasta cooking water.

2 Meanwhile, in a large saucepan, whisk the milk into the cornmeal until smooth. Stir in the mustard, chili powder, and salt, and bring to a simmer over low heat. Stir in the cauliflower and bell pepper, and cook until the pepper is tender, about 5 minutes.

3 Stir in the drained pasta, reserved pasta cooking water, cottage cheese, and Parmesan. Transfer the mixture to a 7 x 11-inch baking dish. Bake uncovered for 20 minutes or until bubbly and golden brown. ***Makes 6 servings***

Curried Mac & Cheese Substitute 2 teaspoons of curry powder for the chili powder. Omit the Parmesan and increase the cottage cheese to 1¾ cups. Stir in ¼ cup of finely chopped storebought mango chutney when adding the cottage cheese in step 3.

Penne Salad with Pecan Pesto

If sugar snaps aren't available, substitute snow peas or green beans. For an even more substantial dish, add 1 cup diced part-skim mozzarella cheese.

per serving	
calories	331
total fat	7.7g
saturated fat	1.9g
cholesterol	5mg
dietary fiber	7g
carbohydrate	53g
protein	14g
sodium	506mg

good source of: beta carotene, folate, selenium, thiamin, vitamin C

3 cloves garlic, peeled
⅓ cup sun-dried tomatoes (not oil-packed)
8 ounces penne pasta
1½ cups packed fresh basil leaves
¼ cup grated Parmesan cheese
1 tablespoon olive oil
1 tablespoon pecan halves
½ teaspoon salt
⅓ cup water
2 red bell peppers, cut into ½-inch squares
½ pound mushrooms, thickly sliced
½ pound sugar snap peas, strings removed

KITCHEN tip

To "blanch" something is to immerse it in boiling water for a minute or so. The reasons for blanching food are many: It can be used to precook the food, set its color, or loosen the skin for peeling. Or, in the case of garlic, blanching is used to reduce its "bite" while preserving its essential pungent flavor.

1 In large pot of boiling water, cook the garlic for 2 minutes to blanch. With a slotted spoon, remove the garlic. Add the sun-dried tomatoes and cook until softened, about 2 minutes. Remove with a slotted spoon and when cool enough to handle, thinly sliver.

2 Bring the water back to a boil. Add the penne and cook according to package directions. Drain and transfer to a large bowl.

3 Meanwhile, in a food processor, combine the garlic, basil, Parmesan, 1 teaspoon of the oil, the pecans, and salt, and process to a smooth puree. Add the water and process until creamy. Pour the dressing over the pasta, tossing to combine.

4 In a large nonstick skillet, heat the remaining 2 teaspoons oil over medium heat. Add the peppers and cook, stirring frequently, until crisp-tender, about 4 minutes. Add the mushrooms and sugar snaps, and cook, stirring frequently, until the sugar snaps are crisp-tender, about 3 minutes.

5 Add the vegetables to the bowl with the pasta. Add the sun-dried tomatoes and toss to combine. Serve at room temperature or chilled. *Makes 4 servings*

All-Vegetable Pizza

per serving	
calories	352
total fat	7.1g
saturated fat	1.6g
cholesterol	0mg
dietary fiber	7g
carbohydrate	56g
protein	16g
sodium	799mg

good source of:
vitamin C

White beans, tomato paste, and garlic are pureed and used to replace the cheese in this delicious pizza. For the least fat, be sure to choose a thin pizza crust.

½ cup water
2 tablespoons balsamic vinegar
½ teaspoon oregano
1 large green bell pepper, cut into rings
1 medium red onion, halved and thinly sliced
6 ounces mushrooms, thinly sliced
1 can (15½ ounces) white beans, rinsed and drained
3 tablespoons tomato paste
2 cloves garlic, peeled
1 large (12 inches) prebaked thin pizza crust
2 teaspoons olive oil

1 Preheat the oven to 450°F.

2 In a large skillet, combine ¼ cup of the water, the vinegar, oregano, bell pepper, onion, and mushrooms over medium heat. Simmer uncovered until the pepper is crisp-tender, about 5 minutes.

3 In a food processor, combine the remaining ¼ cup water, the beans, tomato paste, and garlic, and puree.

4 Place the crust on a large baking sheet and spread the bean mixture over the crust. Scatter the sautéed vegetables over the bean mixture and drizzle with the oil. Bake 15 minutes or until the crust is crisp and the vegetables are hot. *Makes 4 servings*

Mexican-Style Vegetarian Pizza Substitute a can of drained chopped mild green chilies for the green bell pepper. Use pinto beans instead of the white beans and add ½ teaspoon cumin to the bean puree in step 3. Sprinkle the cooked pizza with ¼ cup minced cilantro just before serving.

Rice & Beans Deluxe

1½ cups water
⅔ cup rice
½ teaspoon garlic powder
¼ teaspoon salt
1 can (14½ ounces) stewed tomatoes
1 can (15 ounces) black beans, rinsed and drained
2 cups canned or frozen corn kernels
1 pickled jalapeño pepper, minced
¾ teaspoon cumin
¾ teaspoon coriander
½ cup shredded reduced-fat Cheddar cheese

1 In a medium saucepan, bring the water to a boil over high heat. Add the rice, garlic powder, and salt. Reduce to a simmer, cover, and cook until the rice is tender, about 17 minutes.

2 Meanwhile, in a large saucepan or Dutch oven, combine the tomatoes, black beans, corn, jalapeño, cumin, and coriander, and bring to a boil. Reduce to a simmer, cover, and cook for 2 minutes to heat through.

4 Serve the bean mixture over the rice and sprinkle with the Cheddar.
Makes 4 servings

PER SERVING 333 calories, 3.5g total fat (1.9g saturated), 8mg cholesterol, 9g dietary fiber, 62g carbohydrate, 16g protein, 620mg sodium
Good source of: fiber, folate, thiamin

The only hands-on activity in this ultra-simple recipe (not counting using a can opener) is chopping the jalapeño pepper—a step you can skip if you happen to have canned chopped jalapeños.

Vegetable Curry

per serving	
calories	213
total fat	4.1g
saturated fat	0.6g
cholesterol	0mg
dietary fiber	7g
carbohydrate	40g
protein	7g
sodium	595mg

good source of: beta carotene, potassium, thiamin, vitamin B$_6$, vitamin C

This curry can be varied easily by using different vegetables. Just be sure to substitute vegetables with similar cooking times. For example, a hard vegetable such as rutabaga, winter squash, or parsnip would be a good substitute for the carrots. Soft vegetables, such as mushrooms or yellow squash, could be substituted for the zucchini.

1 pound red potatoes, cut into 1½-inch chunks
1 tablespoon olive oil
2 medium red onions, cut into large chunks
3 cloves garlic, minced
2 teaspoons curry powder
2 carrots, halved lengthwise and cut crosswise into ½-inch-wide slices
2 zucchini (10 ounces total), halved lengthwise and cut crosswise into ½-inch-wide slices
1 cup canned diced tomatoes
1 cup frozen peas
¾ teaspoon salt
¼ cup plain fat-free yogurt

1 In a large saucepan of boiling water, cook the potatoes until tender, about 10 minutes. Drain, reserving ½ cup of the potato cooking liquid.

2 Meanwhile, in a nonstick Dutch oven, heat the oil over medium heat. Add the onions and garlic, and cook, stirring frequently, until the onions are lightly browned, about 10 minutes. Add the curry powder, stirring to coat.

3 Add the carrots and the reserved potato cooking liquid, and cook for 5 minutes. Add the zucchini and cook, stirring frequently, until the carrots are tender, about 5 minutes longer.

4 Add the drained potatoes, tomatoes, peas, and salt, and cook, stirring frequently, until the peas are heated through, about 3 minutes. Stir in the yogurt and serve. ***Makes 4 servings***

Meatless Spaghetti Bolognese

Ragù Bolognese is a pasta sauce typical of the rich cuisine of Bologna, Italy. A traditional ragù is made not only with meat but heavy cream as well—a real health hazard. Here we've captured the richness of the original by using evaporated milk instead of cream, dried mushrooms for a meaty flavor, and TVP (texturized vegetable protein) for the texture of ground meat.

½ cup dried porcini or shiitake mushrooms (½ ounce)
1 cup boiling water
1 tablespoon olive oil
1 small onion, finely chopped
2 carrots, quartered lengthwise and thinly sliced crosswise
3 cloves garlic, minced
1½ cups dried TVP granules
¾ cup dry red wine
¼ cup tomato paste
¾ teaspoon salt
¾ cup evaporated low-fat (1%) milk
10 ounces whole-wheat spaghetti
⅓ cup grated Parmesan cheese

1　In a small heatproof bowl, combine the mushrooms and boiling water; let stand for 20 minutes until softened. Reserving the soaking liquid, scoop out the mushrooms and chop. Strain the liquid through a coffee filter.

2　In a large nonstick skillet, heat the oil over low heat. Add the onion, carrots, and garlic, and cook, stirring frequently, until the carrots are tender, about 10 minutes.

3　Add the mushrooms and TVP to the skillet, stirring to combine. Add the wine and cook until all the liquid has been absorbed, about 4 minutes. Stir in the mushroom soaking liquid and the tomato paste, and cook until the liquid has been absorbed, about 3 minutes.

4　Stir the salt and half of the evaporated milk into the TVP mixture and simmer gently until the milk has been absorbed. Stir in the remaining evaporated milk and simmer 3 minutes, or until the sauce is thick and creamy.

5　Meanwhile, in a large pot of boiling water, cook the spaghetti according to package directions. Drain, reserving ½ cup of the pasta cooking water. Return the pasta to the cooking pot.

6　Stir in the Parmesan. Transfer the sauce to the pasta pot and toss with the pasta and reserved pasta cooking water. *Makes 4 servings*

per serving	
calories	497
total fat	8.8g
saturated fat	3.3g
cholesterol	14mg
dietary fiber	13g
carbohydrate	73g
protein	33g
sodium	801mg

good source of: beta carotene, fiber, magnesium, potassium, riboflavin, selenium, thiamin, zinc

F.Y.I.

TVP is a type of textured soy protein (TSP) made from defatted and dehydrated soy flour. It is available in granular form, which can range from fine to coarse, in health-food stores and in the health-food section in some supermarkets. When rehydrated, TVP absorbs flavors well and has a chewy, meatlike texture.

Spotlite recipe

Pumpkin Couscous Risotto

1½ cups couscous
1 large onion, minced
3 cloves garlic, minced
1 teaspoon sugar
3⅓ cups water
½ cup sherry
¾ teaspoon salt
¾ cup canned unsweetened pumpkin puree
⅓ cup grated Parmesan cheese
¼ teaspoon pepper

1 In a large skillet, heat the couscous over medium heat, stirring frequently, until golden, about 3 minutes. Remove the skillet from the heat.

2 In a large saucepan, combine the onion, garlic, and sugar with ⅓ cup of the water. Cook over medium heat, stirring frequently, until the onion is wilted, about 7 minutes. Stir in the couscous and sherry, and cook until the sherry has evaporated, about 1 minute.

3 In a measuring cup, stir together the remaining 3 cups water and salt. Add the water to the saucepan ½ cup at a time, allowing the couscous to absorb all the liquid before adding any more. Continue cooking and adding liquid until all the liquid has been added and the couscous is creamy.

4 Stir in the pumpkin, Parmesan, and pepper, and cook until heated through, about 3 minutes. *Makes 6 servings*

PER SERVING **226 calories, 2g total fat (1.1g saturated), 4mg cholesterol, 4g dietary fiber, 40g carbohydrate, 9g protein, 401mg sodium**
Good source of: **beta carotene**

Brown Rice & Wild Mushroom Pilaf

Dried porcini can be a bit pricey, so you could make this pilaf with dried shiitake mushrooms instead.

> ½ cup dried porcini mushrooms (½ ounce)
> 2½ cups boiling water
> 2 teaspoons olive oil
> 1 small onion, finely chopped
> ½ pound fresh shiitake mushrooms, stems discarded and
>   caps thinly sliced
> 1 cup brown rice
> ¾ teaspoon salt
> ½ teaspoon rubbed sage
> 1 package (10 ounces) frozen peas, thawed
> ½ cup grated Parmesan cheese

On the *Menu*

This pilaf is intended as a vegetarian main course. Serve it with a salad of chopped, cooked asparagus tossed with a fat-free Italian vinaigrette. To turn this into a nonvegetarian entrée, stir 1 cup of shredded cooked turkey breast or 1 can (6 ounces) drained and flaked water-packed tuna into the pilaf in step 4.

1 In a small heatproof bowl, combine the dried porcini and the boiling water, and let stand for 20 minutes or until softened. Reserving the soaking liquid, scoop out the dried mushrooms and coarsely chop. Strain the soaking liquid through a coffee filter or a paper towel-lined sieve.

2 Preheat the oven to 350°F. In a nonstick Dutch oven, heat the oil over medium heat. Add the onion and cook, stirring occasionally, until the onion is golden brown, about 7 minutes. Add the fresh shiitakes and cook, stirring frequently, until the mushrooms are tender, about 5 minutes.

3 Add the brown rice, stirring to coat. Add the chopped dried mushrooms, the reserved soaking liquid, the salt, and sage, and bring to a boil. Cover, place in the oven, and bake 40 minutes, or until the rice is tender and the liquid has been absorbed.

4 Stir in the peas and Parmesan and return to the oven until the peas are heated through, about 3 minutes. *Makes 4 servings*

F.Y.I.

Cannellini are large white kidney beans often used in Italian cooking. They are sold both dried and canned. Like all canned beans, cannellini should be rinsed and drained before use; this removes much of the sodium present in the canning liquid and also gives the beans a fresher flavor. Look for cannellini in the canned vegetable or Italian foods section of your supermarket.

Cannellini Beans with Rosemary & Parmesan

If you like, toss the beans and sauce with 8 ounces of pasta for a filling vegetarian entree.

1 tablespoon olive oil
½ teaspoon rosemary, minced
5 cloves garlic, minced
1 stalk celery, quartered lengthwise and thinly sliced crosswise
1½ cups canned crushed tomatoes
½ teaspoon pepper
¼ teaspoon salt
2 cans (19 ounces each) cannellini beans, rinsed and drained
2 tablespoons grated Parmesan cheese

1 In a large nonstick saucepan, heat 1 teaspoon of the oil over medium heat. Add the rosemary and garlic, and cook 1 minute. Add the celery and cook until the celery is crisp-tender, about 3 minutes.

2 Stir in the tomatoes, pepper, and salt, and bring to a boil. Add the beans, reduce to a simmer, cover, and cook until the flavors are blended and the beans are rich and creamy, about 5 minutes.

3 Stir in the Parmesan and remaining 2 teaspoons oil. *Makes 4 servings*

Cannellini-Tomato Soup In step 2, stir in 3 cups of Roasted Vegetable Broth or Garlic Broth (*both on page 32*) when adding the tomatoes.

Barley Pilaf with Apricots & Pistachios

Quick-cooking barley is regular barley that has been steamed and rolled prior to packaging. The grain's heart-healthy fiber content remains unchanged.

2 teaspoons olive oil
1 large onion, finely chopped
3 cloves, garlic, minced
1 cup quick-cooking barley
¾ teaspoon salt
½ teaspoon thyme
2⅓ cups water
¼ cup dried apricots, cut into ¼-inch dice
2 tablespoons coarsely chopped shelled pistachios or
    sliced almonds

1 In a medium nonstick saucepan, heat the oil over medium heat. Add the onion and garlic, and cook until the onion is tender and golden brown, about 7 minutes.

2 Add the barley, stirring to combine. Add the salt, thyme, and water, and bring to a boil. Reduce to a simmer, cover, and cook, stirring frequently, until the barley is tender, about 15 minutes.

3 Stir in the apricots and pistachios. *Makes 4 servings*

per serving	
calories	204
total fat	5.1g
saturated fat	0.7g
cholesterol	0mg
dietary fiber	6g
carbohydrate	37g
protein	5g
sodium	441mg

good source of: fiber

Three-Pepper Rice

Three members of the pepper family—spicy dried red chili peppers, dried mild chili peppers (paprika), and fresh red bell peppers—add vitamin C and plenty of flavor to this colorful side dish.

2 teaspoons olive oil
1 large onion, finely chopped
3 cloves garlic, minced
1 teaspoon paprika
¼ teaspoon crushed red pepper flakes
2 large red bell peppers, finely diced
1 cup rice
2 cups water
¾ teaspoon grated orange zest
½ teaspoon salt
¼ cup finely chopped cilantro
2 tablespoons orange juice

1 In a large saucepan, heat the oil over low heat. Add the onion and cook, stirring frequently, until the onion has softened, about 7 minutes. Add the garlic, paprika, and red pepper flakes, and stir to coat.

2 Stir in the bell peppers and cook, stirring frequently, until the peppers have softened, about 5 minutes.

3 Add the rice and stir to coat. Add the water, orange zest, and salt. Bring to a boil, reduce to a simmer, cover, and cook until the rice is tender and creamy, about 17 minutes.

4 Stir in the cilantro until well combined. Remove from heat and stir in the orange juice, fluffing the grains with a fork. ***Makes 4 servings***

Chilied Brown Rice Substitute brown rice for the white (the cooking time will go up to about 45 minutes), and increase the water to 2½ cups. Replace the paprika and red pepper flakes with 1 teaspoon chili powder and ½ teaspoon cumin.

F.Y.I.

Mexican and Indian food would not be the same without cilantro, also called coriander leaf or Chinese parsley. The leaves, which resembles those of flat-leaf parsley (and are in the same botanical family) are strongly aromatic. Cilantro's distinctive flavor is not to everyone's taste—in fact, some researchers believe that there is a genetic component to an individual's reaction to cilantro. If a recipe calls for cilantro and you can't find any fresh, don't bother buying dried cilantro; it has no flavor whatsoever. In fact, you'd be better off substituting fresh basil instead.

Lentil Vegetable Pilaf

Lentils, like other legumes, are packed with protein and are virtually fat-free. They take much less time to cook than dried beans or peas. Lentils are a mainstay of Indian cuisine, and this recipe, made with turmeric and yogurt, has a gentle suggestion of Indian flavors.

> 1 cup lentils
> 3 cups water
> 3 cloves garlic, minced
> ¾ teaspoon salt
> ½ teaspoon turmeric
> 1 cup diced (¼ inch) carrots
> 1 cup canned diced tomatoes
> ¼ cup plain fat-free yogurt

1 In a medium saucepan, combine the lentils, water, garlic, salt, and turmeric, and bring to a boil over high heat. Cover, reduce the heat to low, and simmer 25 minutes.

2 Add the carrots and simmer 5 minutes. Add the tomatoes and simmer until the carrots are tender, about 3 minutes. Remove from the heat and drain any remaining liquid. Stir in the yogurt and serve the lentils hot. *Makes 4 servings*

per serving	
calories	198
total fat	0.6g
saturated fat	0.1g
cholesterol	0mg
dietary fiber	16g
carbohydrate	35g
protein	15g
sodium	550mg

good source of: beta carotene, fiber, folate, magnesium, potassium, thiamin, vitamin B$_6$, vitamin C, zinc

F.Y.I.

Delicate and chewy, wild rice isn't really rice at all, but the seed of an aquatic grass. Still, most people tend to regard wild rice as an exotic form of real rice. Wild rice has more protein than regular rice, and it provides zinc, niacin, and vitamin B_6.

Wild & Brown Rice with Cherries & Walnuts

Since wild rice and brown rice both take about the same amount of time to cook, they make perfect companions in a pilaf. It also helps make such a dish affordable, since wild rice can be quite expensive. The carrot juice adds a slightly sweet flavor and a good amount of beta carotene.

> 2 teaspoons olive oil
> 1 small onion, finely chopped
> 3 cloves garlic, minced
> ¾ cup wild rice
> ⅓ cup brown rice
> 1½ cups carrot juice
> 1½ cups water
> ¾ teaspoon salt
> ½ teaspoon pepper
> ½ teaspoon rosemary, minced
> ½ cup dried cherries, raisins, or dried cranberries
> ⅓ cup coarsely chopped walnuts

1 In a large nonstick saucepan, heat the oil over medium heat. Add the onion and garlic, and cook, stirring frequently, until the onion is tender, about 7 minutes.

2 Add the wild rice and brown rice, stirring to coat. Add the carrot juice, water, salt, pepper, and rosemary, and bring to a boil. Reduce to a simmer, cover, and cook until the rice is tender, about 50 minutes.

3 Stir in the cherries and walnuts. ***Makes 6 servings***

Colcannon

This Irish cabbage-and-potato dish would traditionally be made with green cabbage, but soft, tender Savoy cabbage works particularly well. While all potatoes should be well scrubbed before cooking, these need to be especially clean as they're mashed in their skins.

1½ pounds small all-purpose potatoes, well scrubbed
3 cloves garlic, peeled
1 teaspoon salt
2 tablespoons olive oil
1 large onion, finely chopped
1½ pounds Savoy cabbage, cut into 1-inch chunks (12 cups)
½ teaspoon pepper

1 In a medium saucepan, combine the potatoes, garlic, and cold water to cover. Bring to a boil, reduce to a simmer, partially cover, and cook until the potatoes are tender, about 20 minutes. Drain, reserving ½ cup of the potato cooking liquid.

2 Return the potatoes and garlic to the saucepan. Add ¼ teaspoon of the salt and the reserved potato cooking liquid. With a potato masher, mash the potatoes and garlic until smooth. Set aside.

3 Meanwhile, in a large skillet, heat 1 tablespoon of the oil over medium heat. Add the onion and cook, stirring frequently, until golden brown and tender, about 15 minutes.

4 Add the remaining 1 tablespoon oil, the cabbage, pepper, and remaining ¾ teaspoon salt, and cook, stirring frequently, until the cabbage is tender, about 15 minutes. Stir in the potatoes and cook for 10 minutes to combine the flavors. ***Makes 4 servings***

F.Y.I.

Along with its distinctive flavor, cabbage offers impressive nutritional benefits. It contains natural plant chemicals (phytochemicals) called indoles that appear to lower the risk of hormone-related cancers. Cabbage also has good amounts of vitamin C, folate, and fiber (1 cup of cooked cabbage provides 6.6 g, and uncooked, 7.6 g of fiber), making it a nutritious and heart-healthy food.

Spotlite recipe

Michel Nischan—until recently the Executive Chef at New York City's Heart*beat* restaurant in the W Hotel—creates dishes that stress the pure, natural flavors of food while avoiding such typical restaurant stand-bys as butter and high-fat dairy products. In addition to years of experience in the restaurant world, Chef Nischan has also found inspiration in his personal need to create delicious, low-fat food for his son, Chris, who was diagnosed with juvenile diabetes at the age of five.

Michel Nischan's Root Vegetable & Apple Gratin

¾ pound parsnips, peeled and very thinly sliced
¾ pound potatoes, preferably Yukon gold, peeled and very thinly sliced
2 tablespoons olive oil
1 teaspoon salt
½ teaspoon pepper
1 pound Vidalia onions, halved and thinly sliced
¾ pound sweet potatoes, peeled and very thinly sliced
¾ pound baking apples, such as Cortland or Granny Smith, peeled and thinly sliced
1 tablespoon minced fresh herbs (any combination of parsley, chives, chervil, and thyme)

1 Preheat the oven to 450°F. Spray a 9 x 13-inch baking pan with nonstick cooking spray. Arrange half of the parsnips, in a single layer in the bottom of the pan. Top with half of the potatoes. Drizzle 1 tablespoon of the oil over the potatoes. Sprinkle with ¼ teaspoon each of the salt and pepper.

2 Layer with half the onions and half the sweet potatoes. Sprinkle with ¼ teaspoon of the salt. Top with half the apples.

3 Layer with the remaining parsnips and potatoes and sprinkle with ¼ teaspoon each of the salt and pepper. Top with the remaining onions and sweet potatoes, and sprinkle with the remaining ¼ teaspoon salt. Top with the remaining apples.

4 Drizzle the remaining 1 tablespoon oil over all. Cover tightly with foil. Bake until the vegetables are tender, about 45 minutes. Uncover and sprinkle the herbs on top. Bake 20 minutes, or until the vegetables are lightly browned. Let stand 10 minutes before slicing. ***Makes 8 servings***

PER SERVING 154 calories, 3.7g total fat (0.5g saturated), 0mg cholesterol, 5g dietary fiber, 29g carbohydrate, 3g protein, 301mg sodium
Good source of: **beta carotene, fiber, potassium, vitamin C**

Stir-Fried Italian Rice & Vegetables

If you have leftover rice on hand, use it here. Serve the stir-fry hot, as a side dish, or let it cool to room temperature, toss with olive oil and vinegar, and serve as a rice salad.

1⅓ cups rice
¾ teaspoon salt
4 teaspoons olive oil
1 onion, halved and thinly sliced
5 cloves garlic, slivered
½ pound mushrooms, thinly sliced
2 cups frozen Italian flat beans, thawed and halved crosswise
½ cup chopped fresh basil
½ teaspoon pepper
⅓ cup grated Parmesan cheese

KITCHEN *tip*

Chinese restaurants will usually sell you an order of white rice (or brown rice) to go, shaving a good 20 minutes off the preparation time for this recipe.

1 In a medium saucepan, cook the rice according to package directions, using ¼ teaspoon of the salt.

2 Meanwhile, in a large nonstick skillet, heat the oil over medium heat. Add the onion and garlic, and cook, stirring frequently, until the onion is light golden, about 5 minutes.

3 Add the mushrooms and flat beans, and cook, stirring frequently, until tender, about 5 minutes. Add the rice, basil, the remaining ½ teaspoon salt, and the pepper, and cook, stirring frequently, until the rice is lightly crisped and hot, about 5 minutes. Stir in the Parmesan and serve. ***Makes 6 servings***

Crunchy Baked Potato "Chips"

These are "chips" as in fish and chips, but they're baked, not deep-fried. A combination of breadcrumbs and Parmesan give the potato rounds a crisp, flavorful coating. The chips go especially well with the Balsamic-Ketchup Dipping Sauce (*page 43*).

per serving	
calories	282
total fat	4.5g
saturated fat	1.2g
cholesterol	2mg
dietary fiber	3g
carbohydrate	50g
protein	10g
sodium	425mg

good source of: niacin, potassium, riboflavin, selenium, thiamin, vitamin B$_6$, vitamin C

3 large egg whites
2 tablespoons water
2 teaspoons olive oil
¾ cup plain dried breadcrumbs
2 tablespoons grated Parmesan cheese
¼ cup flour
1½ pounds all-purpose potatoes, cut crosswise into
　　⅓-inch-thick slices
½ teaspoon salt

1 Preheat the oven to 400°F. Spray a large baking sheet with nonstick cooking spray. In a wide, shallow bowl, whisk together the egg whites, water, and oil.

2 In a second shallow bowl, combine the breadcrumbs and Parmesan. In a third bowl, place the flour. Dip the potatoes first in the flour, then in the egg white mixture, then in the breadcrumb mixture, patting the crumbs so they stick to the potatoes.

3 Place the potatoes on the baking sheet and bake until the potatoes are crisp on the outside and cooked through, about 25 minutes. Sprinkle the salt over the potatoes while they're still hot. *Makes 4 servings*

Chili Beans & Peppers

You could make this with any type of canned bean, such as pinto or red kidney. For an even spicier dish, add 1 minced pickled jalapeño pepper, or substitute chipotle pepper sauce for the Louisiana-style hot pepper sauce.

2 teaspoons olive oil
1 large onion, finely chopped
3 cloves garlic, minced
2 green bell peppers, diced
2 cans (15½ ounces each) pink beans, rinsed and drained
2 tablespoons red wine vinegar
2 teaspoons Louisiana-style hot pepper sauce
¾ teaspoon oregano
½ teaspoon salt

ON THE *Menu*

Serve these tart and spicy beans with a simple broiled chicken breast or fillet of fish, along with thick-sliced beefsteak tomatoes sprinkled with minced fresh basil.

1 In a medium nonstick saucepan, heat the oil over medium heat. Add the onion and garlic, and cook, stirring frequently, until the onion is golden brown, about 10 minutes.

2 Add the bell peppers and cook, stirring frequently, until the peppers are tender, about 5 minutes.

3 Stir in the beans, vinegar, hot pepper sauce, oregano, and salt, and bring to a boil. Reduce to a simmer, cover, and cook until the beans are very tender and flavorful, about 15 minutes. ***Makes 4 servings***

Chick-Peas & Red Peppers Use 2 cans (15½ ounces each) chick-peas, rinsed and drained, in place of the pink beans. Use red bell peppers instead of green, and fresh lemon juice instead of the vinegar.

Butternut Squash & Caramelized Onions

Cooking the squash and onions in a large, shallow pan helps them brown, bringing out their natural sweetness.

> 1 butternut squash (about 2 pounds)
> 1 tablespoon sugar
> 2½ teaspoons coriander
> 1 teaspoon oregano
> ¾ teaspoon salt
> 1 large Spanish or Vidalia onion (1 pound), halved and thickly sliced
> 1 tablespoon olive oil

1 Preheat the oven to 450°F. With a large knife, quarter, peel, and seed the squash, and cut crosswise into ½-inch-thick slices.

2 In a large bowl, combine the sugar, coriander, oregano, and salt. Add the squash and onion, and toss well to coat. Add the oil and toss again.

3 Arrange the vegetables on a jelly-roll pan or in a large roasting pan, and bake until the squash is tender and the onion is golden brown, about 45 minutes. Stir several times during cooking. Serve hot or at room temperature. *Makes 4 servings*

Cheese Tortellini with Butternut-Marinara Sauce To turn this vegetable side dish into a meatless main course, prepare the recipe as directed. Then stir the vegetables into 2 cups of bottled marinara sauce and toss with 1 pound of freshly cooked cheese tortellini. Sprinkle with 2 tablespoons of grated Parmesan.

KITCHENtip

Butternut squash can be quite difficult to cut, especially the larger specimens. But there is a way to make it a bit easier. First, be sure you have a big, sturdy knife. Then, cut the squash crosswise at the "waist" —the spot where the squash starts to bulge out. Place the bulbous end on the work surface cut-side down and cut it in half lengthwise. Now you can scoop out the seeds. Cut the narrower end of the squash in half lengthwise, and peel all 4 pieces of squash. Then cut up the squash as directed in the recipe.

Off-the-Shelf

Mushroom-Pesto Mashed Potatoes

Instant mashed potatoes are transformed into a dish worthy of a dinner party (but simple enough for every day) with the addition of dried mushrooms and storebought pesto. Mashed chick-peas add great flavor. The dried mushrooms in this recipe are the mushrooms found in the supermarket in small plastic tubs, simply labeled "Dried Mushrooms." Oddly enough, supermarket dried mushrooms are more expensive than imported dried mushrooms such as porcini. So if you have access to a gourmet store or Italian market, use porcini instead.

½ cup dried mushrooms (½ ounce)
1¼ cups boiling water
1 can (15½ ounces) chick-peas, rinsed and drained
1 cup instant mashed potato flakes
½ teaspoon salt
½ cup fat-free milk
3 tablespoons storebought pesto

1 In a small heatproof bowl, soak the mushrooms in ½ cup of the boiling water until softened, about 10 minutes. Reserving the soaking liquid, scoop out the dried mushrooms and strain the soaking liquid through a coffee filter or a paper towel-lined sieve. (If you are using large mushroom pieces, chop them.)

2 In a large bowl, mash the chick-peas with the reserved mushroom soaking liquid with a potato masher until chunky. Add the remaining ¾ cup boiling water, the instant mashed potato flakes, and the salt, and stir until evenly moistened.

3 Stir in the mushrooms, milk, and pesto, and serve. **Makes 4 servings**

PER SERVING 261 calories, 7.7g total fat (1.6g saturated), 4mg cholesterol, 8g dietary fiber, 34g carbohydrate, 14g protein, 404mg sodium
Good source of: fiber, folate

Spiced Glazed Carrots

How little it takes—warm spices, honey, orange and lemon juices, and a splash of olive oil—to transform carrots from the ordinary to the extraordinary.

4 cups sliced carrots (cut on the diagonal ¼ inch thick)
2 tablespoons honey
1 tablespoon fresh lemon juice
1 tablespoon frozen orange juice concentrate
2 teaspoons olive oil
½ teaspoon salt
¼ teaspoon pepper
¼ teaspoon cinnamon
Large pinch of nutmeg

1 In a large covered skillet, bring 1 inch of water to a boil over high heat. Add the carrots and return to a boil; cover and cook, stirring occasionally, until the carrots are tender, 5 to 6 minutes. Reserving 1 tablespoon of cooking liquid, drain the carrots in a colander.

2 Wipe the skillet dry. Add the reserved cooking liquid, honey, lemon juice, orange juice concentrate, oil, salt, pepper, cinnamon, and nutmeg, and place over medium heat. Cook the mixture, stirring, until heated through.

3 Add the carrots and toss until glazed and heated through. Serve hot. *Makes 4 servings*

per serving	
calories	113
total fat	2.5g
saturated fat	0.4g
cholesterol	0mg
dietary fiber	4g
carbohydrate	23g
protein	1g
sodium	334mg

good source of:
beta carotene, fiber, potassium, thiamin, vitamin B₆, vitamin C

KITCHEN *tip*

Cutting vegetables on the diagonal exposes more of their surface, enabling them to absorb more of the flavor of their cooking liquid. It also helps dense root vegetables, such as carrots, cook more quickly.

Two-Pea Sauté

per serving	
calories	110
total fat	2.8g
saturated fat	0.4g
cholesterol	0mg
dietary fiber	6g
carbohydrate	17g
protein	6g
sodium	377mg

good source of: fiber, folate, magnesium, niacin, riboflavin, thiamin, vitamin B$_6$, vitamin C

Shallots have a delicate flavor caught somewhere between onion and garlic, but subtler than either. Shallots always add a nice touch to dishes, but they can be hard to find, difficult to peel, expensive, or all three. If you'd prefer not to use a shallot here, use 1 scallion, thinly sliced.

2 teaspoons olive oil
1 shallot, minced
1 yellow summer squash (8 ounces), halved lengthwise
  and thinly sliced crosswise
½ pound sugar snap peas, strings removed
1 package (10 ounces) frozen peas
1 teaspoon grated lemon zest
½ teaspoon salt
½ teaspoon tarragon

1 In a large nonstick skillet, heat the oil over medium heat. Add the shallot and cook until tender, about 2 minutes.

2 Add the yellow squash and cook, stirring frequently, until crisp-tender, about 3 minutes.

3 Stir in the sugar snaps, peas, lemon zest, salt, and tarragon, and cook, stirring frequently, until the sugar snaps and squash are tender and the peas are heated through, about 5 minutes. ***Makes 4 servings***

KITCHEN *tip*

Sugar snap peas are completely edible, except for the tough string that runs down the inside (curved) part of the pod. To string a sugar snap, grab the blossom end (the end with the stem) and pull down, as if you were unzipping a zipper. The string should start to pull away from the pod naturally. In larger sugar snaps, there may be a tough string running down the outer side of the pod as well.

Golden Mashed Root Vegetables

per serving	
calories	205
total fat	1.5g
saturated fat	0.9g
cholesterol	4mg
dietary fiber	6g
carbohydrate	44g
protein	5g
sodium	444mg

good source of: beta carotene, fiber, niacin, potassium, thiamin, vitamin B_6, vitamin C

The sweet potatoes and carrots give these mashed root vegetables a lovely golden color. You should mash the vegetables the same way you like your mashed potatoes: smooth or lumpy. Either way, they're delicious. For an interesting flavor dimension, try this vegetable mash with one of the other homemade broths, such as Roasted Vegetable or Garlic, on page 32.

1 pound all-purpose potatoes, peeled and cut into 1-inch chunks
½ pound sweet potatoes, peeled and cut into 1-inch chunks
½ pound carrots, peeled and cut into 1-inch chunks
½ pound white turnips, peeled and cut into 1-inch chunks
½ cup chicken broth, homemade (*page 32*) or reduced-sodium canned
2 tablespoons fat-free milk
2 tablespoons reduced-fat sour cream
1 tablespoon grated Parmesan cheese
½ teaspoon pepper
½ teaspoon salt

1 Place the all-purpose potatoes, sweet potatoes, carrots and turnips in a large saucepan. Add the broth and cold water to cover by 1 inch. Cover and bring to a boil over high heat. Reduce the heat to medium-low and simmer until the vegetables are fork-tender, 15 to 20 minutes. Drain in a colander and return to the cooking pot.

2 Mash the vegetables with the milk. Stir in the sour cream, Parmesan, pepper, and salt. ***Makes 4 servings***

KITCHEN *tip*

The microwave is perfect for "baking" potatoes, though the potato flesh will be a little denser (not as fluffy) than that of conventionally baked potatoes. To microwave, scrub the potatoes well, prick in several places with a fork, and microwave on high power, following your oven's instructions. Two 8-ounce potatoes should take about 12 minutes on high power, plus at least 1 minute of standing time.

Cheese-Stuffed Potatoes with Fresh Salsa

Twice-baked potatoes are a great favorite, and these potato-and-cheese-filled examples are made extra-special (and high in vitamin C) with a topping of fresh tomato salsa.

2 large baking potatoes (8 ounces each)
¼ cup low-fat (1%) cottage cheese
¼ cup low-fat (1.5%) buttermilk
2 tablespoons reduced-fat cream cheese (Neufchâtel)
2 scallions, minced
1 tablespoon minced fresh jalapeño pepper
¼ teaspoon black pepper
¾ pound tomatoes, diced
1 small red bell pepper, diced
⅓ cup minced red onion
3 tablespoons chopped cilantro
1 tablespoon red wine vinegar
½ teaspoon sugar
¼ teaspoon salt

1 Preheat the oven to 450°F. Prick the potatoes in several places. Bake for 45 minutes, or until tender. When cool enough to handle, halve the potatoes lengthwise. With a fork, scrape the potato flesh into a bowl, leaving enough potato attached to the skin to form a sturdy shell (about ⅛ inch). Leave the oven on.

2 Add the cottage cheese, buttermilk, cream cheese, scallions, 1½ teaspoons of the jalapeño pepper, and the black pepper. Mix well to combine, then spoon the mixture into the potato shells. Place the stuffed potato halves on a baking sheet, return to the oven, and bake until the stuffing is piping hot, about 20 minutes.

3 Meanwhile, in a medium bowl, mix together the tomatoes, bell pepper, onion, cilantro, vinegar, sugar, salt, and remaining 1½ teaspoons jalapeño pepper. Serve the potatoes with the salsa spooned on top. *Makes 4 servings*

No-Pork Baked Beans

Mushrooms—both fresh and dried—lend a meaty texture and flavor to this baked cannellini bean side dish.

per serving	
calories	186
total fat	2.4g
saturated fat	0.4g
cholesterol	0mg
dietary fiber	10g
carbohydrate	35g
protein	9g
sodium	400mg

good source of: fiber, folate, magnesium, potassium, thiamin

½ cup dried mushrooms, such as shiitake or porcini (½ ounce)
¾ cup boiling water
1 tablespoon olive oil
1 large onion, finely chopped
½ pound fresh mushrooms, thinly sliced
2 cans (19 ounces each) cannellini beans, rinsed and drained
1 can (15 ounces) crushed tomatoes
3 tablespoons dark brown sugar
2 tablespoons molasses
1½ teaspoons ground ginger

1 In a small heatproof bowl, combine the dried mushrooms and boiling water, and let stand for 20 minutes or until softened. Reserving the soaking liquid, scoop out the dried mushrooms and coarsely chop. Strain the soaking liquid through a coffee filter or a paper towel-lined sieve.

2 Preheat the oven to 375°F. In a nonstick Dutch oven, heat the oil over medium heat. Add the onion and cook, stirring frequently, until tender, about 7 minutes.

3 Add the dried mushrooms, fresh mushrooms, and mushroom soaking liquid, and cook until the mushrooms are tender and the liquid has been absorbed, about 5 minutes.

4 Stir in the beans, tomatoes, brown sugar, molasses, and ginger, and bring to a boil. Cover and transfer to the oven. Bake until the beans are piping hot, about 25 minutes. Uncover and bake until the sauce has thickened somewhat and the beans are glossy, about 10 minutes. ***Makes 8 servings***

per serving	
calories	180
total fat	2.6g
saturated fat	0.4g
cholesterol	0mg
dietary fiber	4g
carbohydrate	36g
protein	2g
sodium	228mg

good source of:
beta carotene, vitamin B_6, vitamin C

F.Y.I.

Pumpkin seed oil is rich in oleic acid and linoleic acid, unsaturated fats that may prevent hardening of the arteries and reduce LDL cholesterol levels in the blood. The oil also contains plant sterols, which are thought to help lower cholesterol. And a recent experimental study on the antioxidant potential of this flavorful oil indicates that it may also help reduce blood pressure.

Roasted Sweet Potato, Apple & Onion Salad

The secret, rich-tasting ingredient in the dressing for this salad is pumpkin seed oil from Austria. However, since it can be hard to come by (it's available in some gourmet food stores), you could use dark sesame oil instead. For a main dish salad, add sliced roast chicken breast or pork tenderloin.

4 teaspoons olive oil
5 cloves garlic, unpeeled
½ teaspoon rosemary, minced
2½ pounds sweet potatoes, peeled and cut into
    ½-inch chunks
3 tablespoons maple syrup
3 tablespoons bourbon or dark rum
¼ cup cider vinegar
2 tablespoons pumpkin seed oil
2 teaspoons Dijon mustard
¾ teaspoon salt
¾ teaspoon pepper
2 large apples, cut into ½-inch chunks
1 large red onion, finely chopped

1 Preheat the oven to 425°F.

2 In a large baking pan, combine the olive oil, garlic, and rosemary. Add the sweet potatoes and toss to coat. Bake, turning the potatoes as they color, for 35 minutes until tender and lightly browned. Remove the garlic from the pan, peel, and mash.

3 Meanwhile, in a large skillet, heat the maple syrup over medium heat. Remove the skillet from the heat and add the bourbon. Return to medium heat and cook for 1 minute. Transfer to a large bowl and whisk in the vinegar, pumpkin seed oil, mustard, salt, pepper, and mashed garlic.

4 Add the apples, onion, and sweet potatoes, and toss to combine. Serve warm, at room temperature, or chilled. *Makes 8 servings*

Lentil, Chick-Pea & Apple Salad

Ever so slightly crunchy and nutty flavored, lentils are a fat-free stand-in for nuts in this salad.

½ cup lentils
3 cloves garlic, minced
1¼ cups plain fat-free yogurt
⅓ cup fresh lemon juice
3 tablespoons light mayonnaise
¾ teaspoon salt
½ cup chopped fresh mint or basil
1 can (15½ ounces) chick-peas, rinsed and drained
3 Granny Smith apples, cut into ½-inch chunks
1 stalk celery, halved lengthwise and thinly sliced
    crosswise

On the *Menu*

Serve this salad as an accompaniment to a simple fish dish, such as Orange-Ginger Salmon (*page 38*). For dessert, offer something light, such as Walnut Meringue Cookies (*page 129*).

1 In a large pot of boiling water, cook the lentils until they are tender but still have a slight chewiness, about 15 minutes. Add the garlic for the last minute of cooking. Drain.

2 Meanwhile, in a large bowl, whisk together the yogurt, lemon juice, mayonnaise, and salt. Stir in the mint.

3 Add the drained lentils (and garlic), the chick-peas, apples, and celery, and stir to combine. Serve at room temperature or chilled. *Makes 6 servings*

Beet, Pear & Endive Salad

Apple juice concentrate and Dijon mustard make a fat-free dressing for this sweet and savory salad.

per serving	
calories	156
total fat	3.8g
saturated fat	0.3g
cholesterol	0mg
dietary fiber	5g
carbohydrate	31g
protein	3g
sodium	457mg

good source of: fiber

¼ cup frozen apple juice concentrate
4 teaspoons Dijon mustard
1 tablespoon cider vinegar
¼ teaspoon salt
¼ teaspoon pepper
1 can (15 ounces) whole beets, cut into ½-inch chunks
1 pound Bartlett pears (about 2), quartered and thinly sliced
2 Belgian endives, thinly sliced crosswise
3 tablespoons coarsely chopped walnuts

1 In a large bowl, whisk together the apple juice concentrate, mustard, vinegar, salt, and pepper.

2 Add the beets, pears, and endive, and toss to combine. Serve the salad with the walnuts sprinkled on top. **Makes 4 servings**

Beet, Apple & Fennel Salad Use 1 pound of crisp red apples in place of the pears. Use 2 cups sliced fresh fennel instead of the endive. And sprinkle with chopped toasted almonds instead of walnuts.

per serving	
calories	57
total fat	3g
saturated fat	0.4g
cholesterol	0mg
dietary fiber	2g
carbohydrate	7g
protein	3g
sodium	250mg

good source of:
folate, thiamin, vitamin B$_6$, vitamin C

KITCHEN *tip*

The best-quality asparagus spears are firm yet tender, with deep green or purplish tips that are closed and compact; partially open and wilted tips are the most obvious signs of aging. Though some people prefer very thin asparagus (often called "pencil grass"), while others prefer the thicker stalks, the size of asparagus is not an indication of its quality. Whatever size you choose, however, the spears will cook more evenly if they are uniform in size.

Asparagus Vinaigrette

This Asian-inspired vinaigrette works equally well with green beans, sugar snap peas, or snow peas.

1½ pounds asparagus, cut into 2-inch pieces
⅓ cup fresh lemon juice
2 tablespoons water
1 tablespoon Dijon mustard
2 teaspoons dark sesame oil
½ teaspoon tarragon
¼ teaspoon salt
1 small red bell pepper, diced

1 In a vegetable steamer, cook the asparagus until crisp-tender, about 3 minutes. Drain well. Arrange the asparagus on a serving platter.

2 In a medium bowl, whisk together the lemon juice, water, mustard, oil, tarragon, and salt. Stir in the bell pepper. Spoon the vinaigrette over the asparagus. ***Makes 4 servings***

Asparagus & Potatoes Vinaigrette Steam the asparagus as directed, but place in a large salad bowl instead of on a platter. In a medium pot of boiling water, cook 1 pound of small red potatoes until tender, about 20 minutes. When cool enough to handle, thickly slice and add to the asparagus. Double the vinaigrette, and add to the warm vegetables along with the bell pepper. Toss well.

Pickled Pepper & Cabbage Salad

per serving	
calories	120
total fat	2.8g
saturated fat	0.4g
cholesterol	0mg
dietary fiber	5g
carbohydrate	24g
protein	2g
sodium	162mg

good source of: beta carotene, fiber, folate, potassium, thiamin, vitamin B_6, vitamin C, vitamin E

If coleslaw is the first thing that comes to mind when you have cabbage on hand, try this wilted cabbage salad instead. A low-fat celery seed dressing cooks with shredded cabbage, bell peppers, and onions to give them a fresh, tart-sweet flavor.

¼ cup apple cider vinegar
¼ cup water
3 tablespoons sugar
¼ teaspoon celery seed
¼ teaspoon salt
¼ teaspoon black pepper
2 teaspoons olive oil
4 cups shredded cabbage
3 large red bell peppers, cut into thin strips
1 medium onion, halved and thinly sliced

1 In a small saucepan, combine the vinegar, water, sugar, celery seed, salt, and black pepper. Bring to a boil over high heat, stirring to dissolve the sugar. Reduce the heat to medium-low and simmer 5 minutes. Remove from the heat.

2 In a very large nonstick saucepan, heat the oil over medium-high heat. Add the cabbage, bell peppers, and onion, and toss gently to mix. Sauté, tossing the vegetables often, until they begin to soften and cook down, 6 to 7 minutes.

3 Stir in the vinegar mixture and bring to a boil. Cover, reduce the heat to medium-low, and cook, tossing occasionally, until the vegetables are very tender, 6 to 8 minutes.

4 Serve warm, at room temperature, or chilled. *Makes 4 servings*

Cabbage & Green Pepper Salad For a visually opposite effect, use red cabbage instead of green, and green pepper instead of red.

Asparagus & Lentil Salad with Tomato-Lemon Dressing

Asparagus and lentils, two folate-packed ingredients, make a delicious salad when combined and tossed in a tomato-lemon dressing. The wasabi in the dressing adds a pleasingly "hot" note to this room-temperature salad.

1 cup lentils

2 pounds asparagus, trimmed and cut into 1-inch lengths (5 cups)

1 can (5.5 ounces) spicy tomato-vegetable juice

3 tablespoons fresh lemon juice

2 tablespoons olive oil

1 tablespoon Dijon mustard

1 tablespoon prepared wasabi paste

¾ teaspoon salt

1 pint cherry tomatoes, halved

1 large red onion, diced

8 cups shredded spinach

1 In a large pot of boiling salted water, cook the lentils 15 minutes. Add the asparagus to the pot and cook until the asparagus are crisp-tender and the lentils are tender, 2 to 3 minutes.

2 Meanwhile, in a large bowl, whisk together the tomato-vegetable juice, lemon juice, oil, mustard, wasabi paste, and salt. Add the lentil mixture and toss well. Let cool to room temperature. Add the tomatoes, onion, and spinach, and toss again. ***Makes 6 servings***

F.Y.I.

Wasabi is the pungent, sinus-clearing green paste that comes with sushi or sashimi in Japanese restaurants. You can buy wasabi powder or paste in the supermarket, though this is not actually made from true wasabi—what you are actually getting is Western-style horseradish that has been tinted green to resemble real wasabi. This is because true wasabi—which is botanically related to horseradish—is an extremely difficult, and thus expensive, plant to grow.

KITCHEN tip

Not all apples are suitable for baking. Some varieties have such a soft texture or so thin a skin that if you baked them, they would simply collapse into a heap. Rome and Cortland are two classic "baking apples." But there are lots of apple varieties out there, so it may be a matter of experimentation to find other types that work well for baking. Some apples that are not good bakers are McIntosh, Red Delicious, and Macoun.

Baked Apples with Date-Nut Stuffing

If you can't find dates, use regular or golden raisins instead.

½ cup old-fashioned rolled oats
⅓ cup pitted dates, finely chopped
3 tablespoons maple syrup
2 tablespoons coarsely chopped walnuts
4 large baking apples, such as Rome or Cortland
   (8 ounces each)
¾ cup apple juice

1 Preheat the oven to 350°F. In a medium bowl, combine the oats, dates, maple syrup, and walnuts.

2 Core each apple from the stem end going down to within ½ inch of the blossom end. With a vegetable peeler, remove ¾ inch of the peel around the opening created by the corer at the stem end. Stuff the date-nut mixture into the hollow core of each apple. Place in a baking dish just large enough so the apples fit snugly in a single layer.

3 Pour the apple juice into the baking pan. Cover with foil and bake, basting the apples with the pan juices once, for 50 minutes, or until the apples are soft and tender but not falling apart. Serve drizzled with the pan juices.
Makes 4 servings

Chocolate-Flecked Angel Food Cake

Serve a slice of cake with a scoop of frozen yogurt and fresh strawberries or raspberries.

1 cup cake flour
1⅓ cups granulated sugar
12 large egg whites, at room temperature
1 teaspoon cream of tartar
¼ teaspoon salt
1½ teaspoons vanilla extract
¼ teaspoon almond extract
6 tablespoons mini chocolate chips (3 ounces)
2 teaspoons confectioners' sugar

KITCHEN *tip*

Angel food cakes are cooled upside down in the pan to keep the soufflé-like cake from collapsing as it cools. Many angel food cake pans have three "legs" on their rim to support the pan when it's turned upside down. But if you're using a pan without legs, you can invert the cake pan over the neck of a bottle. Use a glass bottle, preferably a full one to counterbalance the weight of the cake.

1 Preheat the oven to 350°F. Have a long-necked bottle ready to hang the cake on as it cools. On a sheet of waxed paper, sift together the flour and ⅓ cup of the granulated sugar. Set aside.

2 In a large bowl, with an electric mixer, beat the egg whites, cream of tartar, and salt until soft peaks form. Gradually beat in the remaining 1 cup granulated sugar, 1 tablespoon at a time, until very stiff peaks form. Beat in the vanilla and almond extracts until well combined.

3 Sift the flour-sugar mixture over the egg white mixture and sprinkle the chocolate chips lightly over the top, then fold into the egg whites.

4 Pour the batter into an ungreased 10-inch angel food cake pan or tube pan and bake 1 hour, or until the cake is golden brown and pulls away from sides of pan. Cool the cake upside down in the pan set over the neck of a bottle.

5 Loosen the sides of the cake with a metal spatula and invert onto a cake plate. Using a fine-mesh sieve, dust the cake with the confectioners' sugar.
Makes 10 servings

F.Y.I.

Almond milk is made by crushing almonds, steeping them in water, then straining and pressing them to extract their liquid. Manufacturers generally add vitamins and minerals, such as vitamin D and calcium. Almond milk is also high in vitamin E. It can be found in health-food stores, packed in aseptic containers. You can also make your own almond milk: Grind almonds in a food processor, add cold water to cover, and let stand for 30 minutes. Strain, pushing on the solids to extract as much liquid as possible.

Creamy Almond Rice Pudding

We've taken rice pudding, that most comforting of desserts, and made it dairy-free by using almond milk, which suffuses the rice (nutty-tasting jasmine or basmati) with sweet almond flavor. If you prefer, substitute low-fat (1%) dairy milk for the almond milk.

½ cup jasmine or basmati rice
3 cups almond milk (almond beverage)
¼ cup sugar
¼ teaspoon salt
⅓ cup dark or golden raisins
¼ teaspoon almond extract

1 In a large saucepan, combine the rice and water to cover. Bring to a boil and boil 5 minutes. Drain.

2 Return the rice to the pan. Add the almond milk, sugar, and salt, and bring to a boil over medium heat. Reduce to a simmer and cook, uncovered, stirring frequently for 30 minutes.

3 Add the raisins and continue to cook, stirring frequently, until the rice is tender and the pudding is thick, about 10 minutes.

4 Remove from the heat and let cool to room temperature. Stir in the almond extract. Serve at room temperature or chilled. *Makes 4 servings*

Strawberry-Rhubarb Compote

Though hothouse rhubarb is available much of the year, locally grown farmers' market rhubarb is still a great way to celebrate the end of winter (rhubarb is one of the first plants up in the spring). Serve this compote by itself or over low-fat frozen yogurt.

I stick of cinnamon
3 whole cloves
2 allspice berries
½ cup sugar
3 large stalks rhubarb, cut into ¾-inch lengths (2½ cups)
I pint strawberries, halved (2 cups)
I tablespoon chopped fresh ginger
2 tablespoons water

I   Tie the cinnamon, cloves, and allspice in a small piece of cheesecloth. In a nonaluminum saucepan, combine the sugar, rhubarb, strawberries, ginger, water, and the spice bag. Stir until well combined. Bring to a boil.

2   Reduce to a simmer, cover, and cook until the rhubarb is just tender but has not begun to disintegrate, 10 to 15 minutes. Remove and discard the spice bag. ***Makes 4 servings***

Rhubarb-Cherry Compote Although rhubarb and strawberries are classic companions, you could also make this with fresh cherries instead of strawberries. Use 2 cups of pitted sweet cherries, but coarsely chop them so they will cook in the same amount of time as the rhubarb (cherries are denser than strawberries).

per serving	
calories	233
total fat	1.9g
saturated fat	1g
cholesterol	6mg
dietary fiber	3g
carbohydrate	49g
protein	7g
sodium	84mg

good source of: calcium, potassium, riboflavin, vitamin B$_{12}$, vitamin C

KITCHEN *tip*

If you don't have the whole spices called for in this compote, you can use ground versions in their place. For the cinnamon stick, substitute ½ teaspoon ground. If you don't have whole cloves, use ⅛ teaspoon ground. If you don't have allspice berries, use ⅛ teaspoon ground. No need to tie the ground spices in cheesecloth; just add them to the saucepan as is.

Baked Spiced Carrot Pudding

This delicious cross between a pudding and a cake is exotically flavored with dark roasted sesame oil and cardamom.

½ cup packed brown sugar
1¼ cups carrot juice
2 large egg whites
2 tablespoons dark sesame oil
1¾ cups shredded carrots (½ pound)
1 cup flour
1 teaspoon baking powder
¼ teaspoon baking soda
¾ teaspoon cinnamon
1 teaspoon ground ginger
¾ teaspoon cardamom
¼ teaspoon salt
⅔ cup golden raisins

1 Preheat the oven to 400°F. Spray a 9-inch square glass baking dish with nonstick cooking spray.

2 In a large bowl, whisk together the brown sugar, carrot juice, egg whites, and sesame oil until well combined. Stir in the carrots.

3 In a separate bowl, stir together the flour, baking powder, baking soda, cinnamon, ginger, cardamom, and salt. Fold the flour mixture into the carrot mixture. Fold in the raisins.

4 Set the baking dish in a larger pan. Pour the pudding mixture into the baking dish and pour hot water into the larger pan to come halfway up the sides of the baking dish. Bake until the pudding shrinks from the sides of the pan, about 35 minutes. Serve warm. ***Makes 8 servings***

F.Y.I.

Native to India, cardamom is an aromatic, sweet spice (reminiscent of lemon, mint, and pine with hints of pepper) that is used in many cuisines, from Indian to Scandinavian. You can purchase whole cardamom pods (though not usually in supermarkets), the hulled seeds, or ground cardamom.

per serving	
calories	265
total fat	7.6g
saturated fat	0.8g
cholesterol	0mg
dietary fiber	4g
carbohydrate	48g
protein	4g
sodium	150mg

good source of: selenium, thiamin, vitamin E

KITCHEN *tip*

Adding a little bit of lemon juice to a pastry crust helps make it tender. This is especially important with reduced-fat crusts, such as the one for this Apple-Apricot Pie.

Apple-Apricot Pie

How often have you eaten a pie with a light, flaky bottom crust? Probably not often. Luckily, this can work to your health advantage: If you make a pie with no bottom crust—like this one—you can have a low-fat pie without sacrificing the flavor of the crust. If you don't have walnut oil, use all olive oil in the crust.

Filling:
½ cup apricot all-fruit spread
2 tablespoons sugar
2 tablespoons fresh lemon juice
2½ pounds apples, peeled and cut into 1-inch wedges
¾ cup dried apricots, diced
3 tablespoons flour
¾ teaspoon cinnamon

Crust:
1¼ cups flour
3 tablespoons toasted wheat germ
2 tablespoons sugar
¾ teaspoon salt
¼ cup extra-light olive oil
3 tablespoons ice water
1 tablespoon fresh lemon juice

1 Preheat the oven to 425°F. Make the filling: In a large bowl, combine the fruit spread, sugar, and lemon juice. Add the apples, apricots, flour, and cinnamon, and toss to combine. Arrange the filling in a 9-inch pie plate.

2 Make the crust: In a large bowl, combine the flour, wheat germ, sugar, and salt. In a small bowl, whisk together the olive oil, ice water, and lemon juice until well combined. Make a well in the center of the flour mixture. Add the oil mixture and stir with a fork until well combined. Shape the dough into a ½-inch-thick disk.

3 Roll the dough out between 2 sheets of lightly floured waxed paper into an 11-inch circle (⅛ inch thick). Remove the top sheet of waxed paper and invert the dough over the apples. With your fingers, crimp the edges of the dough. With a sharp knife, cut several short slashes in the middle of the crust to act as steam vents. Transfer the pie to a jelly-roll pan.

4 Bake for 15 minutes. Reduce the heat to 375°F and bake 30 minutes, or until the crust is golden brown and the apples are bubbly. (If the crust begins to overbrown, loosely tent with a piece of foil.) Transfer to a rack to cool slightly. Serve the pie with a spoon, as you would a cobbler. *Makes 8 servings*

Spotlite recipe

Apple-Cranberry Sauce

4 large Granny Smith apples, unpeeled, cut into large
   chunks
1⅓ cups fresh or frozen cranberries
½ cup frozen apple juice concentrate
1 tablespoon sugar

1 In a medium saucepan, combine the apples, cranberries, apple juice concentrate, and sugar. Bring to a boil over medium heat. Reduce to a gentle simmer and cook until the apples are slightly chunky but soft, about 10 minutes.

2 Using an immersion blender, blend the apple-cranberry mixture until not quite smooth, with some chunkiness. Serve at room temperature or chilled. *Makes 4 servings*

PER SERVING 147 calories, 0.2g total fat (0g saturated), 0mg cholesterol, 4g dietary fiber, 39g carbohydrate, 1g protein, 11mg sodium
Good source of: fiber, potassium, vitamin C

An immersion blender (also called a hand blender) is an indispensable kitchen tool—especially if you like applesauce. All you have to do is cook up the apples and then use the immersion blender to puree them right in the pan. If you like your applesauce chunky, just blend one-half to two-thirds of the cooked apples.

Walnut Meringue Cookies

Toasted oats underscore the nutty flavor of the walnuts in these crisp cookies, giving them lots of flavor without much fat.

per cookie	
calories	44
total fat	1g
saturated fat	0.2g
cholesterol	0mg
dietary fiber	0g
carbohydrate	8g
protein	1g
sodium	25mg

⅔ cup old-fashioned rolled oats
⅓ cup walnuts
4 large egg whites, at room temperature
¼ teaspoon salt
1 cup sugar
1 teaspoon vanilla extract
3 tablespoons mini chocolate chips (1 ounce)

1 Preheat the oven to 300°F. Line 2 large baking sheets with foil or parchment paper. In a 7 x 11-inch baking pan, toast the oats for 10 minutes, or until golden brown and crisp. Transfer the toasted oats to a food processor. Add the walnuts and pulse until the oats are finely ground. Set aside.

2 In a large bowl, with an electric mixer, beat the egg whites and salt until foamy. Gradually add the sugar, 1 tablespoon at a time, beating until stiff peaks form. Beat in the vanilla. Gently fold in the oat-walnut mixture and chocolate chips.

3 Drop the batter by rounded tablespoons, 1 inch apart, onto the lined baking sheets. Bake for 1 hour, switching the baking sheets from top to bottom shelf midway through, until the cookies are crisp and golden brown. Transfer the cookies to a wire rack to cool. ***Makes 32 cookies***

KITCHEN *tip*

Beating egg whites when they're at room temperature gives them greater volume.

Chocolate-Raspberry Buttermilk Cupcakes

Raspberries and chocolate have a natural affinity, but cherry jam or orange marmalade would work equally well here.

1¼ cups flour
3 tablespoons unsweetened cocoa powder
1 teaspoon baking powder
½ teaspoon baking soda
½ teaspoon cinnamon
¼ teaspoon salt
¼ cup extra-light olive oil
½ cup packed light brown sugar
1 large egg
1 teaspoon vanilla extract
⅓ cup buttermilk
½ cup seedless raspberry jam
1 tablespoon confectioners' sugar

1 Preheat the oven to 375°F. Line twelve 2½-inch muffin-tin cups with paper liners.

2 In a medium bowl, combine the flour, cocoa powder, baking powder, baking soda, cinnamon, and salt.

3 In a large bowl, with an electric mixer, beat the oil and brown sugar until light and fluffy. Add the egg and vanilla, and beat until well combined. On low speed, alternately beat in the flour mixture and the buttermilk, beginning and ending with the flour mixture.

4 Spoon one-third of the batter into the muffin cups. Make a small well in the batter of each cupcake. Dividing evenly, spoon the raspberry jam into each well. Spoon the remaining batter evenly over the raspberry jam. Bake 20 minutes, or until the tops of the cupcakes spring back when lightly touched. Turn the cupcakes out onto a wire rack to cool completely.

5 Dust the tops of the cooled cupcakes with confectioners' sugar before serving. ***Makes 12 cupcakes***

KITCHEN *tip*

Buttermilk, because of its acid content, helps to break down the gluten in flour, making for a tender "crumb" in baked desserts. This is especially helpful in low-fat baking. If you don't have buttermilk, you can make a quick "soured" milk as a stand-in. For 1 cup, place 1 tablespoon lemon juice or white vinegar in a liquid measuring cup. Add enough low-fat (1%) milk to measure 1 cup.

Fresh Grape Gelatin

per serving	
calories	136
total fat	1.5g
saturated fat	1.1g
cholesterol	5mg
dietary fiber	1g
carbohydrate	28g
protein	4g
sodium	25mg

good source of:
vitamin B_6

There are plenty of reasons to make your own gelatin desserts: fresher flavors, no additives, less sugar. Consider the fact that you can't buy a gelatin dessert made with red grape juice, and you'll be convinced.

2 envelopes unflavored gelatin
3 cups red grape juice
½ cup plain fat-free yogurt
½ cup reduced-fat sour cream
3 tablespoons sugar
1 cup seedless red grapes, halved
1 banana, thinly sliced

1 In a large saucepan, sprinkle the gelatin over the grape juice. Let stand until softened, about 2 minutes. Bring to a simmer over low heat and simmer very gently until the gelatin has dissolved, about 3 minutes. Remove from the heat and let cool to room temperature.

2 Meanwhile, in a medium bowl, whisk together the yogurt, sour cream, and sugar. Pour one-third of the juice mixture into the yogurt mixture and whisk until well combined.

3 Place the yogurt mixture and the remaining juice mixture in the refrigerator until the mixtures are just beginning to firm up, but are not set, about 45 minutes (depending on how efficient your refrigerator is; check the gelatin after 30 minutes).

4 Fold the grapes and bananas into the juice mixture. Then fold in the yogurt mixture. Spoon into 8 custard cups and refrigerate until set and chilled, about 3 hours. ***Makes 8 servings***

F.Y.I.

The skins of red and purple grapes contain a substance called resveratrol. Animal studies indicate that resveratrol may lower LDL cholesterol and have anticlotting effects.

Pumpkin Crème Brûlée

For many dessert lovers, crème brûlée is the ultimate indulgence, but one that they feel guilty about because of its formidable fat content. If you are a crème brûlée lover, you are in luck with this recipe. Low-fat milk replaces the cream and the number of egg yolks has been reduced, but the thick, rich texture of pumpkin puree makes up the difference.

3 large eggs
2 large egg whites
⅓ cup granulated sugar
¼ teaspoon salt
2 cups low-fat (1%) milk
½ teaspoon cinnamon
⅛ teaspoon allspice
⅛ teaspoon ground cloves
⅛ teaspoon ground white pepper
½ teaspoon vanilla extract
⅔ cup canned unsweetened pumpkin puree
⅓ cup packed light brown sugar

1 In a medium bowl, whisk together the whole eggs, egg whites, granulated sugar and salt.

2 In a medium saucepan, combine the milk, cinnamon, allspice, cloves, and white pepper. Bring to a simmer over medium heat. Whisking constantly, add about 1 cup of the hot milk to the egg mixture to warm it. Then stir the warmed egg mixture back into the pan and continue cooking, stirring constantly, until the mixture coats the back of a spoon, about 10 minutes. Remove from the heat and stir in the vanilla. Cover and let stand at room temperature for 20 minutes.

3 Preheat the oven to 350°F. Gently whisk the pumpkin puree into the custard mixture until well combined but not frothy and pour into six 8-ounce ramekins or custard cups. Line the bottom of a baking pan (large enough to comfortably hold all the ramekins) with paper towels and place the ramekins on top. Pour boiling water to come halfway up the sides of the ramekins and bake until the custard is set but still slightly wobbly, about 45 minutes. Cool on a wire rack, then refrigerate.

4 Just before serving time, preheat the broiler. Place the brown sugar in a fine-mesh sieve and sprinkle the tops of the custards evenly. Place the custards on a baking sheet and broil 6 inches from the heat until the tops have caramelized, 2 to 3 minutes. Watch the custards carefully so they don't burn. Cool for several minutes before serving. *Makes 6 servings*

per serving	
calories	176
total fat	3.4g
saturated fat	1.3g
cholesterol	110mg
dietary fiber	1g
carbohydrate	30g
protein	7g
sodium	194mg

good source of: beta carotene, riboflavin, selenium, vitamin B$_{12}$

KITCHEN *tip*

To check whether a custard is done, dip a spoon into it. If the custard coats the spoon evenly, it's ready. You can test it further by drawing a line across the custard-coated spoon with your finger. If it leaves a track (instead of closing up), it's thick enough.

Apple & Date Crisp

Unsweetened yogurt provides a pleasing contrast to the natural sweetness of this fruit crisp. Instead of the more usual cinnamon, the fruit here is flavored with a combination of cardamom and clove.

per serving	
calories	324
total fat	9.2g
saturated fat	1.2g
cholesterol	1mg
dietary fiber	6g
carbohydrate	61g
protein	5g
sodium	30mg

½ cup flour
½ cup old-fashioned rolled oats
¼ cup packed light brown sugar
¼ cup sliced almonds
¼ cup extra-light olive oil
6 McIntosh apples (2¼ pounds), peeled and cut into
    ½-inch chunks
1½ cups pitted dates, coarsely chopped
½ cup apple cider
½ teaspoon ground cardamom
⅛ teaspoon ground cloves
1½ cups plain fat-free yogurt

1 Preheat the oven to 350°F. In a small bowl, toss together the flour, oats, brown sugar, almonds, and oil until the mixture resembles coarse meal.

2 In a 9-inch square glass baking dish, toss together the apples, dates, cider, cardamom, and cloves. Spoon the oat topping over the fruit. Bake 45 minutes, or until the fruit is soft and tender and the topping is golden brown and crisp.

3 Serve the fruit crisp warm, at room temperature, or chilled, and topped with yogurt. *Makes 8 servings*

per serving	
calories	263
total fat	9.9g
saturated fat	3.7g
cholesterol	51mg
dietary fiber	3g
carbohydrate	32g
protein	11g
sodium	307mg

good source of: beta carotene, riboflavin, selenium, thiamin, vitamin E

On the *Menu*

Because cheesecake—even a slimmed-down, nutrient-dense cake like this one—is an indulgence, it should follow a light and low-fat main course. Try broiled flounder, steamed sugar snap peas, and brown rice.

Pumpkin Cheesecake with Oat-Walnut Crust

This luscious reduced-fat cheesecake, with a crust full of nutritional goodies, is really a very creamy pumpkin pie that easily could become a favorite on Thanksgiving or any special family dinner.

⅔ cup old-fashioned rolled oats
½ cup walnuts
½ cup toasted wheat germ
2 tablespoons plus 1 cup packed light brown sugar
1 package (8 ounces) reduced-fat cream cheese (Neufchâtel)
1 package (8 ounces) fat-free cream cheese
15 ounces firm silken tofu
1 can (16 ounces) unsweetened pumpkin puree
2 large eggs
2 large egg whites
2 tablespoons dark rum or bourbon
1½ teaspoons vanilla extract
1½ teaspoons cinnamon
1 teaspoon allspice
1 teaspoon ground ginger
½ teaspoon salt

1 Preheat the oven to 350°F. Place the oats and walnuts on a baking sheet and bake 5 minutes until lightly toasted. Transfer to a food processor. Add the wheat germ and 2 tablespoons of the brown sugar and pulse until finely ground. Transfer to a 9-inch springform pan and press the mixture into the bottom of the pan.

2 In the food processor (no need to clean the bowl), combine the cream cheese, tofu, pumpkin puree, whole eggs, egg whites, rum, vanilla, cinnamon, allspice, ginger, salt, and remaining 1 cup brown sugar and process until smooth. Pour the batter into the springform pan.

3 Bake 1 hour. Turn the oven off, prop the oven door open slightly, and let the cake stand 45 minutes in the turned-off oven. Let cool to room temperature, then chill overnight before serving. ***Makes 12 servings***

Wine-Poached Plums with Yogurt Cream

If you don't have a cinnamon stick, you can make this with ground cinnamon. Use ½ teaspoon and add it in step 2, when you heat the wine mixture.

½ cup plain fat-free yogurt
2 tablespoons reduced-fat sour cream
1 cup dry red wine
⅓ cup sugar
1 cinnamon stick, split lengthwise
3 strips (3 x ½-inch) orange zest
¼ cup orange juice
6 red plums, halved and pitted
½ teaspoon vanilla extract

1 In a small bowl, combine the yogurt and sour cream. Cover and refrigerate until serving time.

2 In a medium saucepan, combine the wine, sugar, cinnamon, orange zest, and orange juice. Bring to a boil over medium heat, reduce to a simmer, and add the plums. Cook, turning once, until the plums are tender, about 10 minutes.

3 With a slotted spoon, transfer the plums to a serving bowl. Return the wine mixture to the heat and bring to a boil. Cook, stirring occasionally, until the liquid has reduced to ¾ cup, about 10 minutes. Let cool to room temperature and discard the orange zest. Stir in the vanilla.

4 Pour the syrup over the plums. Chill the plums in the syrup for at least 1 hour and up to 3 days. Spoon the plums and syrup into 4 dessert bowls and top with a dollop of the yogurt cream. ***Makes 4 servings***

F.Y.I.

Citrus zest is the thin, outermost colored part of the rind of citrus fruits that contains the strongly flavored oils. Zest imparts an intense flavor to desserts, dressings, and marinades. Use a vegetable peeler to remove strips of zest; be careful to remove only the colored layer, not the spongy white pith beneath it.

Spotlite recipe

Buttermilk Waffles with Apple-Raisin Topping

½ cup pineapple juice concentrate
2 Granny Smith apples, unpeeled, cut into wedges
½ cup raisins
½ teaspoon cinnamon
¼ cup flaxseeds
½ cup whole-wheat flour
¼ cup all-purpose flour
2 tablespoons yellow cornmeal
1 tablespoon light brown sugar
2 teaspoons baking powder
¼ teaspoon salt
1 large egg, separated, plus 2 large egg whites
1 cup buttermilk

1 In a large skillet, bring the pineapple juice concentrate and ¼ cup water to a boil over high heat. Add the apples, raisins, and cinnamon, and cook, stirring occasionally, until the apples are tender, about 5 minutes. Remove from the heat and let cool to room temperature.

2 In a mini food processor or coffee mill, grind the flaxseeds to the consistency of coarse flour. Transfer to a large bowl and add the whole-wheat flour, all-purpose flour, cornmeal, brown sugar, baking powder, and salt.

3 In a small bowl, combine the egg yolk and buttermilk. In a large bowl, beat the 3 egg whites until stiff peaks form. Make a well in the flour mixture and stir in the buttermilk mixture. Gently fold in the beaten whites.

4 Spray a nonstick waffle iron with nonstick cooking spray. Preheat the iron. Spoon ½ cup batter per waffle into the iron and cook until golden brown and crisp. Repeat with the remaining batter to make a total of 8 waffles. Serve warm with the apple-raisin topping. **Makes 4 servings**

PER SERVING 366 calories, 5.6g total fat (1.1g saturated), 55mg cholesterol, 8g dietary fiber, 71g carbohydrate, 12g protein, 378mg sodium
Good source of: fiber, potassium, riboflavin, selenium, thiamin

Shiitake-Tofu Scramble

While this recipe serves two, it can easily be doubled, but you'll need a 10-inch skillet. If you prefer, substitute button mushrooms for the shiitake.

1 large egg
4 large egg whites
¼ teaspoon thyme
¼ teaspoon salt
¼ teaspoon black pepper
1 teaspoon olive oil
¼ cup minced scallion
¼ cup diced red bell pepper
3 ounces firm tofu, diced (about ½ cup)
2 fresh shiitake mushrooms, stems discarded and caps
    coarsely chopped
2 tablespoons grated Parmesan cheese

1 In a small bowl, beat together the whole egg, egg whites, thyme, salt, and black pepper.

2 In an 8-inch nonstick skillet, heat the oil over medium heat. Add the scallion, bell pepper, tofu, and shiitake, and cook, stirring, until the tofu is just beginning to brown, about 2 minutes.

3 Add the beaten egg mixture. Immediately sprinkle on the Parmesan and cook, stirring with a wooden spoon, until the eggs form soft curds, 1 to 2 minutes. *Makes 2 servings*

per serving	
calories	165
total fat	7.9g
saturated fat	2.5g
cholesterol	111mg
dietary fiber	1g
carbohydrate	7g
protein	16g
sodium	567mg

good source of:
riboflavin, selenium, vitamin B_{12}, vitamin C, vitamin D, zinc

Super Heart-Smart Müesli Mix

A Swiss doctor (named Bircher-Benner) who ran a diet clinic in Switzerland in the late 19th century, invented a breakfast dish that included oats, chopped apples, and soured cream. A packaged version of the original Bircher-müesli mix has been marketed for years (and is still a tradition in Switzerland), and usually contains dried fruit instead of the fresh fruit in the original. For our müesli, we've chosen high-fiber figs and dates, as well as heart-smart sunflower seeds.

4 cups old-fashioned rolled oats
½ cup (3 ounces) dried figs, finely diced
½ cup (3 ounces) pitted dates, finely diced
½ cup raisins
½ cup (3 ounces) dried apricots, finely diced
⅓ cup hulled sunflower seeds
⅓ cup packed light brown sugar

1 Preheat the oven to 400°F. On a jelly-roll pan, toast the oats until golden brown and fragrant, stirring once, 7 to 10 minutes. Transfer to a large bowl and let cool to room temperature.

2 Add the figs, dates, raisins, apricots, sunflower seeds, and brown sugar. Store in an airtight container. ***Makes about 6 cups***

F.Y.I.

Just about every ingredient in this müesli recipe will help to protect your health. You'll receive an impressive amount of cholesterol-reducing soluble fiber from the oats, dried figs, dates, raisins, and apricots. The sunflower seeds provide folate, iron, selenium, vitamin B$_6$, vitamin E, zinc, protein, and fiber as well as linoleic acid, an unsaturated fat.

Corn & Egg Burritos

Using one whole egg gives the scrambled eggs in these breakfast burritos richness and flavor, but without a lot of added cholesterol and fat.

⅓ cup water
2 large red bell peppers, diced
4 scallions, thinly sliced
½ cup low-fat (1%) milk
3 tablespoons flour
1 cup frozen corn kernels, thawed
4 low-fat flour tortillas (8 inches)
1 large egg
5 large egg whites
½ teaspoon salt
¼ cup shredded jalapeño jack cheese

1 In a large nonstick skillet, bring the water to a boil over medium heat. Add the bell pepper and scallions, and cook, stirring frequently, until the pepper is tender, about 5 minutes.

2 Meanwhile, in a small bowl, whisk the milk into the flour until smooth. Add the flour mixture to the skillet and cook, stirring frequently, until the mixture is slightly thickened, about 2 minutes. Reduce the heat to low and stir in the corn.

3 Preheat the oven to 400°F. Wrap the tortillas in foil, place in the oven, and heat for 5 minutes, or until warmed through.

4 In a medium bowl, whisk together the whole egg, egg whites, and salt. Pour the egg mixture into the vegetable mixture and cook, stirring constantly, until the eggs are just set but still creamy, about 4 minutes. Stir in the cheese. Unwrap the tortillas, spoon the scrambled eggs on top, and roll up. *Makes 4 servings*

KITCHEN tip

It is actually cheaper to buy whole eggs and throw away the yolks than it is to buy one of the egg substitutes on the market. For example, one egg's worth of egg substitute or packaged egg whites costs in the neighborhood of 40 cents per egg. An equal volume of egg whites from a regular carton of eggs costs only 12 cents an egg.

HOMEMADE
breakfast smoothies

Smoothies were born sometime in the late 1960s or early 1970s when yogurt was a newfangled health food for most Americans. Since then, these yogurt-based shakes have become a part of this country's culinary tradition, in part, perhaps, because Americans have a fondness for food designed to eat on the go. Although smoothies make a good snack any time of day, they are an especially convenient solution for people who are tempted to skip breakfast. To save time, you could combine all of the ingredients—except the ice cubes—in the jar of a blender the night before. Cover and refrigerate the blender jar. Then in the morning, add the ice cubes and make the smoothie.

Pineapple-Peach Smoothie

¾ cup peach or mango nectar

½ cup chunks of fresh or juice-canned pineapple

¼ cup plain fat-free yogurt

1½ teaspoons honey

3 ice cubes

In a blender, combine all of the ingredients and puree until thick and smooth. **Makes 1 serving**

PER SERVING: 196 CALORIES, 0.4G TOTAL FAT (0G SATURATED), 1MG CHOLESTEROL, 2G DIETARY FIBER, 49G CARBOHYDRATE, 3G PROTEIN, 48MG SODIUM. **GOOD SOURCE OF:** VITAMIN C

Tangerine Smoothie

¼ cup frozen orange-tangerine or tangerine juice concentrate

½ cup low-fat (1%) milk

1½ teaspoons malted milk powder

3 ice cubes

In a blender combine all of the ingredients and puree until thick and smooth. **Makes 1 serving**

PER SERVING: 207 CALORIES, 2.3G TOTAL FAT (1.3G SATURATED), 7MG CHOLESTEROL, 1G DIETARY FIBER, 41G CARBOHYDRATE, 7G PROTEIN, 116MG SODIUM. **GOOD SOURCE OF:** CALCIUM, FOLATE, POTASSIUM, RIBOFLAVIN, THIAMIN, VITAMIN B_{12}, VITAMIN C

Banana-Peanut Smoothie

1 banana (6 ounces), cut into large chunks

½ cup fat-free milk

1 tablespoon honey

1 tablespoon chocolate syrup

1½ teaspoons creamy peanut butter

2 ice cubes

In a blender, combine all the ingredients and puree until thick and smooth. **Makes 1 serving**

PER SERVING: 307 CALORIES, 4.9G TOTAL FAT (1.3G SATURATED), 2MG CHOLESTEROL, 4G DIETARY FIBER, 63G CARBOHYDRATE, 8G PROTEIN, 114MG SODIUM. **GOOD SOURCE OF:** POTASSIUM, RIBOFLAVIN, VITAMIN B_6

Breakfast Fruit Sundaes

per serving	
calories	179
total fat	1.1g
saturated fat	0.1g
cholesterol	1mg
dietary fiber	5g
carbohydrate	44g
protein	3g
sodium	21mg

good source of: fiber, potassium, vitamin B$_6$, vitamin C

Sundaes for breakfast? Why not? But instead of ice cream, this fresh fruit sundae is served with a honey-sweetened fat-free yogurt.

½ cup plain fat-free yogurt
3 tablespoons honey
½ teaspoon grated lime zest
1 tablespoon fresh lime juice
1 pint strawberries, halved
2 kiwifruit, peeled and thinly sliced crosswise
1 cup blueberries
2 small plums, cut into ½-inch wedges
1 banana, thinly sliced

1 In a small bowl, stir together the yogurt, 1 tablespoon of the honey, and the lime zest. Refrigerate the honey-yogurt until serving time.

2 In a large bowl, combine the remaining 2 tablespoons honey and the lime juice. Add the strawberries, kiwi, blueberries, plums, and banana, and toss to combine. Serve the fruit (and the juices that accumulate) topped with the honey-yogurt. *Makes 4 servings*

KITCHEN *tip*

Pancake batter usually includes whole eggs, which is what helps the pancake puff up as it cooks. To enhance the lightness of these pancakes, egg whites only (to reduce cholesterol and saturated fat) are beaten until they hold a peak, and then folded into the batter.

Raspberry Whole-Grain Pancakes

Flaxseeds—which are high in healthful fats and fiber—add a nutty flavor to the pancakes. For more information on flaxseeds, see Buttermilk Waffles with Apple-Raisin Topping on page 136.

1 tablespoon flaxseeds
1 cup whole-wheat flour
½ cup all-purpose flour
2 tablespoons light brown sugar
2½ teaspoons baking powder
½ teaspoon salt
3 large egg whites
1¼ cups fat-free milk
2 tablespoons nonfat dry milk powder
1 cup raspberries
3 teaspoons extra-light olive oil

1 In a mini food processor, spice grinder, or coffee mill, process the flaxseeds until finely ground. Transfer to a large bowl and stir in the whole-wheat flour, all-purpose flour, brown sugar, baking powder, and salt.

2 In a medium bowl, beat the egg whites until stiff peaks form. In a small bowl, stir the milk into the milk powder until smooth. Make a well in the center of the flour mixture and stir in the milk mixture. Fold in the beaten egg whites. Gently fold in the raspberries.

3 In a large nonstick skillet, heat 1 teaspoon of the oil over medium-low heat. Using a ¼-cup measure, drop the batter into the pan to make 4 pancakes and cook until the tops begin to bubble, about 2 minutes. Carefully turn the pancakes over and cook 30 seconds longer or until set.

4 Repeat with the remaining oil and pancake batter to make a total of 12 pancakes. ***Makes 4 servings***

per serving	
calories	351
total fat	4.7g
saturated fat	2g
cholesterol	42mg
dietary fiber	3g
carbohydrate	70g
protein	9g
sodium	302mg

good source of: ribo-flavin, thiamin, vitamin B$_{12}$

Cinnamon Apple-Raisin Bread Pudding

If you like, substitute cinnamon-raisin bread for the white bread and omit the cinnamon and raisins from the pudding.

    1 pound McIntosh or Cortland apples, cut into ½-inch
        cubes
    ⅓ cup raisins
    ½ cup apple cider or juice
    ⅔ cup packed dark brown sugar
    2¼ cups low-fat (1%) milk
    ¼ cup reduced-fat sour cream
    1 large egg
    1 large egg white
    1 teaspoon vanilla extract
    1 teaspoon grated lemon zest
    ½ teaspoon cinnamon
    8 ounces white sandwich bread (about 8 slices), toasted
        and torn into large pieces

1 Preheat the oven to 350°F.

2 In a large skillet, combine the apples, raisins, and cider. Bring to a boil over medium heat, reduce to a simmer, cover, and cook until the apples have soft-ened, about 5 minutes.

3 Meanwhile, in a large bowl, whisk together the brown sugar, milk, sour cream, whole egg, egg white, vanilla, lemon zest, and cinnamon.

4 Place the toast pieces in an 8-cup glass or ceramic baking dish along with the apple mixture. Pour the milk-egg mixture on top and bake for 25 min-utes, or until the custard is just set and the top is golden brown. Serve warm or at room temperature. **_Makes 6 servings_**

Dried Fruit & Bran Bread

Start with bran muffin mix, add some dried fruit and chopped nuts, and you can make a tasty loaf in no time. Using pineapple juice as the liquid adds a nice hint of natural sweetness and moisture to the loaf.

1 package (7 ounces) bran muffin mix
¼ cup flour
1 package (7 ounces) mixed dried fruit, coarsely
   chopped
¼ cup coarsely chopped walnuts
¾ cup pineapple juice
2 large egg whites

1 Preheat the oven to 400°F. Spray a 9 x 5-inch loaf pan with nonstick cooking spray.

2 In a large bowl, stir together the bran muffin mix, flour, fruit, and walnuts. Make a well in the center of the mixture and add the pineapple juice and egg whites. Stir to combine.

3 Spoon the batter into the pan and bake for 35 minutes, or until a toothpick inserted in the center comes out clean. Cool 10 minutes in the pan, then invert onto a wire rack to cool completely. ***Makes 8 slices***

PER SLICE **215 calories, 5.6g total fat (0.9g saturated), 0mg cholesterol, 5g dietary fiber, 40g carbohydrate, 4g protein, 205mg sodium**
Good source of: **fiber**

Tofu Salmon Spread

Perfect for breakfast or brunch, this spread is great on crisp toast, bagels, or pita bread.

per 2 tablespoons	
calories	33
total fat	1.8g
saturated fat	0.3g
cholesterol	1mg
dietary fiber	1g
carbohydrate	1g
protein	4g
sodium	196mg

good source of: calcium, omega-3 fatty acids

1 teaspoon unflavored gelatin
2 tablespoons cold water
15 ounces firm tofu, cut into large pieces
4 ounces smoked salmon, cut into large pieces
2 teaspoons grated lemon zest
2 tablespoons fresh lemon juice
¾ teaspoon salt
2 scallions, thinly sliced
2 tablespoons capers, coarsely chopped if large

1 In a small heatproof bowl, sprinkle the gelatin over the cold water and let stand until softened, about 2 minutes. Place the bowl in a pan of simmering water and let sit until the gelatin has dissolved, about 1 minute. Set the mixture aside to cool slightly.

2 In a food processor, combine the tofu, smoked salmon, lemon zest, lemon juice, salt, and gelatin mixture, and puree until smooth.

3 Add the scallions and capers, and pulse until combined. Chill 1 hour before serving. ***Makes 3 cups***

Whole Wheat Walnut-Raisin Bread

Like many whole-wheat bread recipes, this one also contains all-purpose flour for a lighter texture. Let your mind go blank as you knead the dough—it's a tried-and-true stress-buster. If you like, shape the dough into 2 small loaves rather than 1 large loaf. Note, however, that the baking time may be slightly less.

¾ cup golden raisins
2 tablespoons honey
2 cups lukewarm water (105° to 115°F)
1 package (¼ ounce) active dry yeast
2¾ cups whole-wheat flour
2 cups all-purpose flour
2 teaspoons salt
1 cup walnut halves, coarsely chopped

1 In a small bowl, combine the raisins and ⅓ cup hot tap water. Set aside to soften.

2 In a large mixing bowl, stir together the honey and ½ cup of the lukewarm water. Add the yeast and stir to dissolve. Let stand until foamy, about 5 minutes. Stir in the remaining 1½ cups lukewarm water.

3 Add the whole-wheat flour, 1½ cups of all-purpose flour, and the salt, stirring until well combined. Stir in enough of the remaining all-purpose flour so that the dough leaves the sides of the bowl.

4 Turn the dough onto a floured surface and knead 5 to 10 minutes, adding more flour if necessary, until the dough is smooth, elastic, and slightly sticky.

5 Place the dough in a lightly oiled large mixing bowl, turning to coat. Cover with a damp cloth and set aside in a warm place to rise until doubled in bulk, about 1½ hours. Lightly oil a large baking sheet.

6 Punch the dough down and turn onto a floured surface. Drain the raisins and pat dry with paper towels. Knead the raisins and walnuts into the dough. Shape into 1 large round loaf and place on the baking sheet. Cover with a damp cloth and let rise until almost doubled, about 30 minutes.

7 Preheat the oven to 425°F. With a paring knife, slash the top of the loaf. Bake for 15 minutes. Reduce the oven temperature to 375°F and bake for 30 minutes, or until the loaf is nicely browned and the bottom sounds hollow when tapped. Cool on a rack before slicing. ***Makes 16 slices***

per slice	
calories	182
total fat	3.6g
saturated fat	0.4g
cholesterol	0mg
dietary fiber	4g
carbohydrate	34g
protein	6g
sodium	293mg

good source of: niacin, selenium, thiamin

F.Y.I.

Because they are dried and contain little of the water that is in the original fruit, raisins are a concentrated source of nutrients (as well as calories and sugar). These sweet dried fruits are rich in iron and potassium, and soluble and insoluble fiber.

Dried Plum & Toasted Oat Muffins

per muffin	
calories	182
total fat	4.7g
saturated fat	0.8g
cholesterol	18mg
dietary fiber	2g
carbohydrate	32g
protein	4g
sodium	219mg

good source of:
selenium

Dried plums (prunes) are always available, but in fresh plum season, you can make these with diced firm-ripe plums. The best type of fresh plum to use would be a so-called prune plum, because its flesh is quite dense and not too wet.

1¼ cups old-fashioned rolled oats
1 cup flour
½ cup packed light brown sugar
2 teaspoons baking powder
½ teaspoon baking soda
½ teaspoon salt
¼ teaspoon allspice
1 cup buttermilk
3 tablespoons extra-light olive oil
1 large egg
1 cup pitted dried plums (6 ounces), diced

1 Preheat the oven to 400°F. Line 12 muffin cups with paper liners. Place the oats in a baking pan and bake, stirring once, until toasted and lightly browned, about 10 minutes. Transfer to a food processor and pulse until finely ground.

2 Transfer the oats to a large bowl and stir in the flour, brown sugar, baking powder, baking soda, salt, and allspice.

3 In a medium bowl, stir together the buttermilk, oil, and egg. Make a well in the center of the oat mixture and pour in the buttermilk mixture, stirring until just combined. Fold in the dried plums. Do not overmix.

4 Spoon the batter into the muffin cups. Bake 15 to 17 minutes, or until the muffins are golden and a toothpick inserted in the center comes out clean. Remove from the pan and cool on a wire rack. ***Makes 12 muffins***

THE SAVVY SHOPPER

canadian bacon Canadian bacon isn't really bacon at all; it's lean smoked pork, similar to ham. Since Canadian bacon is precooked, it can be used as is; but for extra flavor, sauté it briefly—just until crisped around the edges. A very small amount of Canadian bacon (as little as 1 ounce) adds big flavor to dishes, but with much less fat than regular bacon.

capers Capers are the flower buds of a small bush found in Mediterranean countries. The buds are dried and then pickled in vinegar with some salt. Capers come in a range of sizes from the smallest, usually labeled "nonpareil" (which means "unequaled" in French), to capers the size of raisins. Because capers have such an intense flavor, and a lot of sodium, you should use them in small quantities and also rinse them before using to remove some of the salt. If all you can find are the larger capers, chop them a bit so that they will spread through the dish more evenly.

carrot juice Carrot juice is a much overlooked ingredient. Most people think of it as a "health" drink and not as a cooking ingredient. It is, however, a wonderful substitute for broth in soups, stews, sauces, marinades, and can also be used in baked goods. Its subtle natural sweetness brings out the flavors in savory dishes. It also adds a spectacular amount of the antioxidant beta carotene. Canned carrot juice, available in supermarkets, has the highest concentration of beta carotene. The refrigerated carrot juice found in supermarkets and health-food stores is lower in beta carotene, but still a healthful option.

coriander, ground The tiny, round, yellow-tan seeds of the coriander plant have no flavor resemblance to the plant's leaves (which are commonly called cilantro). Coriander comes both as whole seeds and ground. Pungently spicy, yet sweet and slightly citrusy, coriander is a key component in curries and is often used in spice cakes and cookies.

cumin The seed of a plant in the parsley family, nutty-flavored whole or ground cumin seeds are often a component of chili powder; indeed, the spice is commonly used to flavor many Mexican and Tex-Mex dishes. Cumin is also a key ingredient in curry powder. To bring out its flavor, lightly toast cumin before adding it to a dish.

curry powder Curry powder is not one spice but a blend of spices, commonly used in Indian cooking to flavor a dish with sweet heat. It also adds a characteristic yellow-orange color. While curry blends vary (consisting of as many as 20 spices and herbs), they typically include turmeric (for its vivid yellow color), fenugreek, ginger, cardamom, cloves, cumin, coriander, and cayenne pepper. Commercially available Madras curry is hotter than other store-bought types.

ginger, fresh When shopping for fresh ginger, look for knobs with plump, smooth, somewhat shiny skin. If the skin is wrinkled or cracked, the ginger is past its prime. When preparing ginger, if the skin is thin, it is not necessary to peel it. Fresh ginger should be stored in the refrigerator. If you've bought more than you'll need in a couple of weeks, you can freeze the whole piece of ginger. Then when you need to use it, just chop, slice, or grate it.

ginger, ground Ground ginger is a "warm" spice made by drying and pulverizing gingerroot. A standard ingredient in spicy desserts, ginger is used in savory dishes as well as in baking. Ground ginger is not, however, a substitute for fresh ginger. Like all spices, ginger loses its flavor with time; buy a new jar if the ginger in your spice rack lacks a lively bite.

hot pepper sauce Once upon a time, if you told someone to buy hot pepper sauce, you could be confident that they would come home with a red Louisiana-style hot sauce with the tang of vinegar. Now there is a world of hot sauces, with heat levels and blends of ingredients that vary considerably from one brand to another. There are, however, a couple of styles of hot sauce that are fairly consistent: For example, in addition to the red Louisiana-style sauces, there are green jalapeño-based sauces, Caribbean-style sauces (which are sweet-sour and often include fruit), and super-hot Jamaican hot sauces (which are yellow because they are made with yellow mustard and hot because they're made with Scotch Bonnet chili peppers). There are also garlicky Southeast Asian sauces.

ketchup Until recently, ketchup was a garden-variety American condiment. But with the publicity over the plant pigment called lycopene, which is believed to have healthful properties, ketchup—a good source

of lycopene—has moved into the spotlight. This has resulted in a variety of flavored ketchups, but it has also meant the arrival of "no-salt-added" ketchup, which is a good compromise between the fairly high-sodium regular ketchup and the rather bland low-sodium ketchup.

lentils, red These small salmon-colored lentils are sold hulled, which makes them cook more quickly than the larger brown or green lentils. You will find red lentils in many supermarkets, usually where regular lentils are sold. But they are also reliably found in Indian and Middle Eastern markets.

molasses Molasses is a by-product of the refining of sugarcane or sugar beets. Molasses is available in various grades: Light molasses comes from the first boiling of the sugar syrup in the sugar-refining process and is the type of molasses most commonly found in supermarkets. Dark molasses is the second boiling of the sugar syrup and has a much darker, more pronounced flavor. Blackstrap molasses comes from the third boiling and is the strongest and most bitter.

mushrooms, shiitake Grown for hundreds of years only in Asia, shiitake mush-

rooms are now cultivated in this country. They have a meaty texture and very mushroomy flavor. Only the caps of the mushrooms are edible; the stems get discarded. Dried shiitakes are also available; they may be sold as shiitakes or, if you buy them in an Asian market, they may be called Chinese black mushrooms. Like other dried mushrooms, shiitakes must be reconstituted in hot water before using.

oil, dark sesame The sesame oil most commonly found in supermarkets is a dark, polyunsaturated oil, pressed from toasted sesame seeds. Since it is often used in Asian cuisines, and because many brands of this oil have Asian-sounding names, cookbooks often refer to it as "Asian sesame oil," but in the store you will not find any labels that say this. The label is more likely to just say "sesame oil" or sometimes "roasted sesame oil." You will also find cold-pressed sesame oil in health-food stores; this type of oil is not from toasted sesame seeds, and is light in both flavor and color. The dark oil breaks down when heated, so it is not used for sautéing, but rather as a seasoning, added at the end of cooking.

THE SAVVY SHOPPER

pizza crust, prebaked
Prebaked pizza crusts are certainly a boon to the busy cook. They come with a range of fat and sodium levels, depending on the brand. The best choice is to buy thin crust so you can maximize the nutrition of the pizza you make by concentrating on healthful toppings and not worrying about the calories from a thick crust.

sage This native Mediterranean herb is most familiar as a seasoning for poultry stuffing. Sold as whole leaves (fresh or dried), rubbed (crumbled), and ground, sage has a bold, rather musty flavor and aroma. Try it with any type of poultry, or with pork, veal, or ham. Or use it in cheese sauces; in bean or vegetable soups and seafood chowders; or with cooked mushrooms, lima beans, peas, tomatoes, or eggplant.

soy sauce Soy sauce is a condiment made from fermented soybeans, roasted grain (wheat, barley, or rice are common), and salt. Traditional soy sauce is quite high in sodium and should be used sparingly. Most supermarkets carry reduced-sodium (about one-third less sodium than the traditional) and "lite" (about 50% less sodium) versions. Just be careful if you shop for soy sauce in an Asian market, because there is a type of Chinese soy sauce called "Light," a designation that does not refer to sodium content but to a certain style of soy sauce. Chinese light soy sauce is actually higher in sodium than regular soy sauce.

tofu Tofu (also known as "soybean curd") is an exceptionally nutritious food. It is a good source of soy protein and isoflavones, both of which have promising health benefits. Tofu is made by curdling soymilk with a calcium or magnesium salt. (When tofu is made with calcium salt, calcium becomes an essential nutrient in the finished product. However, not all tofu is made with a calcium salt. If you are looking to get calcium from the tofu you eat, you do need to read the label.) There are two basic styles of tofu: regular and silken. Both regular and silken tofu come in degrees of firmness (a function of how much water is left in the tofu): soft, firm, and extra-firm. There is also "lite" tofu, which is lower in calories and fat. Check the label carefully to make sure that you are purchasing the specific variety of tofu that will suit your culinary needs. For example, extra-firm tofu is best used for marinating and cutting into cubes for a stir-fry. Softer tofus are best for desserts or other foods that require a wetter consistency.

tortillas Tortillas are round, thin, flexible Mexican flatbreads. They come in two basic varieties: corn and flour. Corn tortillas are made of a special corn flour called masa harina and water, and no added fat. They are usually about 6 to 7 inches in diameter. Flour tortillas, on the other hand, are made of wheat flour and, traditionally, lard (American supermarket versions are usually made with vegetable shortening). The principal difference between corn and flour tortillas—not counting taste—is that flour tortillas tend to be much more flexible. This is why flour tortillas are often used to make burritos and sandwich wraps. Flour tortillas come in a wide range of sizes, from 6 inches in diameter up to 10 inches, and sometimes bigger. The bigger flour tortillas are sometimes sold as "burrito-style" tortillas. Flour tortillas are also marketed in a variety of flavors, such as jalapeño or sun-dried tomato or basil. Although the downside to flour tortillas is their fat content, there are low-fat versions available.

Leading Sources of

fiber

food	calories	fiber (g)
†Black beans, cooked, 1 cup	227	15
†Chick-peas, cooked, 1 cup	269	12.5
†Baby lima beans, cooked, 1 cup	189	10.8
†Green peas, cooked, 1 cup	134	8.8
Raspberries, 1 cup	60	8.4
Bulgur, cooked, 1 cup	151	8.2
Blackberries, 1 cup	75	7.6
†Baked sweet potato, with skin, 8 oz	279	7.3
†Oat bran, ½ cup	116	7.2
†Dried figs, 3 medium	145	7.0
Dried pears, ½ cup	236	6.8
Artichoke, 1 medium	60	6.5
Whole-wheat pasta, cooked, 1 cup	174	6.3
Wheat bran, ¼ cup	31	6.2
†Dried plums (prunes), ½ cup	203	6.0
†Barley, cooked, 1 cup	193	6.0
†Dried apricots, ½ cup	155	5.9
Butternut squash, cooked, 1 cup	82	5.7
Baked potato, with skin, 8 oz	247	5.4
†Carrots, cooked, 1 cup	70	5.1
Buckwheat groats, cooked, 1 cup	155	4.5
†Hass avocado, ½ medium	153	4.2
Pear, 1 fresh	98	4.0
†Oatmeal, cooked, 1 cup	145	4.0
Blueberries, 1 cup	81	3.9
Almonds, roasted, 1 oz	166	3.9
Sunflower seeds, ¼ cup	205	3.8
†Apple, with skin, 1 medium	81	3.7
Wheat germ, toasted, ¼ cup	108	3.6
Brown rice, cooked, 1 cup	216	3.5
Strawberries, 1 cup	43	3.3
†Carrots, 1 cup grated raw	47	3.3
Mushrooms, cooked, 1 cup	48	2.4
Grapefruit, ½ medium	39	1.3

†Foods particularly high in soluble fiber.

folate

food	calories	folate (mcg)
Lentils, cooked, 1 cup	230	358
Black-eyed peas, cooked, 1 cup	200	358
Pinto beans, cooked, 1 cup	234	294
Chick-peas, cooked, 1 cup	269	282
Spinach, cooked, 1 cup	41	263
Asparagus, cooked, 1 cup	43	263
Black beans, cooked, 1 cup	227	256
Kidney beans, cooked, 1 cup	225	230
Green soybeans, cooked, 1 cup	254	200
Chicory, raw, chopped, 1 cup	41	198
Collard greens, cooked, 1 cup	49	177
Turnip greens, cooked, 1 cup	29	170
Romaine lettuce, chopped, 2 cups	16	152
Fortified oatmeal, cooked, 1 cup	105	151
Beets, diced, cooked, 1 cup	75	136
Split peas, cooked, 1 cup	231	127
Spinach, raw, chopped, 2 cups	13	116
Orange juice, 1 cup	112	109
Broccoli, cooked, 1 cup	44	94
Brussels sprouts, cooked, 1 cup	61	94
White rice, enriched, cooked, 1 cup	205	92
Florida avocado, ½ medium	170	81
Broccoli, cooked, 1 cup	44	78
Green peas, cooked, 1 cup	111	76
Okra, cooked, 1 cup	51	73
Sunflower seeds, 1 oz	162	64
Hass avocado, ½ medium	153	57
Wheat germ, toasted, 2 tablespoons	54	50

Leading Sources of

calcium

food	calories	calcium (mg)
Tofu, firm (made with calcium sulfate), 3 oz	123	581
Yogurt, plain, fat-free, 1 cup	137	488
Yogurt, plain, low-fat, 1 cup	155	448
Milk, nonfat dry powder, ⅓ cup	109	411
Milk, fat-free, 1 cup	100	352
Parmesan cheese, 1 oz	111	335
Ricotta cheese, part-skim, ½ cup	170	335
Sardines, canned (with bones), 3 oz	177	325
Milk, low-fat (1%), 1 cup	102	300
Cheddar cheese, reduced-fat, 1 oz	81	253
Collard greens, cooked, 1 cup	49	226
Salmon, canned (with bones), 3 oz	130	203
Mozzarella cheese, part-skim, 1 oz	72	183
White beans, cooked, 1 cup	249	161

potassium

food	calories	potassium (mg)
Baked potato, with skin, 8 oz	220	844
Spinach, cooked, 1 cup	41	839
Prune juice, 1 cup	182	707
Flounder, cooked, 5 oz	145	622
Yogurt, plain, low-fat, 1 cup	155	573
Hass avocado, ½ medium	153	548
Salmon fillet, cooked, 5 oz	292	544
Tomato juice, 1 cup	41	535
Salmon, canned (with bones), 5 oz	217	534
Cantaloupe, 1 cup cubes	56	494
Orange juice, 1 cup	112	473
Banana, 1 medium	109	467
Broccoli, cooked, 1 cup	44	456
Tuna, water-packed, 6-oz can	220	408
Milk, low-fat (1%), 1 cup	102	381
Grapefruit juice, 1 cup	101	336
Romaine lettuce, 2 cups chopped	16	325
Apricots, 3 fresh	50	311
Kale, cooked, 1 cup	36	296
Pumpkin seeds, roasted, 1 ounce	126	261
Shrimp, cooked, 5 oz	140	258
Turkey breast, cooked, 3 oz	115	248
Orange, 1 medium	62	237
Chicken breast, cooked, 3 oz	140	218
Sunflower seeds, 1 oz	162	195

magnesium

food	calories	magnesium (mg)
Kasha, cooked, 1 cup	685	438
Quinoa, uncooked, ½ cup	318	179
Spinach, cooked, 1 cup	41	157
Swiss chard, cooked, 1 cup	35	151
Sunflower seeds, ¼ cup	205	127
Cocoa powder, ¼ cup	49	107
Millet, cooked, 1 cup	286	106
Baby lima beans, cooked, 1 cup	189	101
Halibut, cooked, 3 oz	119	91
Wheat bran, ¼ cup	31	89
Almonds, roasted, 1 oz	166	86
Brown rice, cooked, 1 cup	216	84
Pumpkin seeds, roasted, 1 oz	126	74
Amaranth leaves, cooked, 1 cup	28	73
Artichoke, 1 medium	60	72
Tuna, fresh, cooked, 3 oz	118	54
Chocolate chips, ¼ cup	201	48

Leading Sources of

unsaturated fats*

type of oil	% MUFA	% PUFA
Sunflower oil	84	4
Hazelnut oil	78	10
Olive oil	74	8
Avocado oil	71	13
Almond oil	70	17
Canola oil	59	30
Pistachio oil	49	33
Peanut oil	46	32
Sesame oil	40	41
Corn oil	24	59
Walnut oil	23	63
Flaxseed oil	17	69
Safflower oil	12	75
Soybean oil	11	45

*Cooking and salad oils vary in their percentages of fatty acids. The oils above are ranked according to their monounsaturated fatty acid percentages, with their polyunsaturated levels also listed.

vitamin B_{12}

food	calories	vitamin B_{12} (mcg)
Clams, steamed, ½ doz	40	26.73
Oysters, cooked, ½ doz	47	14.34
Alaskan king crab, cooked, 3 oz	82	9.78
Sardines, 3 oz	177	7.60
Trout, cooked, 3 oz	144	4.23
Ground beef, extra-lean, cooked, 3 oz	192	2.57
Beef, top round, cooked, 3 oz	184	2.28
Lamb, loin, cooked, 3 oz	253	2.11
Tuna, water-packed, 6-oz can	218	1.99
Yogurt, plain, fat-free, 1 cup	137	1.50
Milk, nonfat dry powder, ⅓ cup	109	1.25
Scallops, cooked, 3 oz	91	1.13
Milk, fat-free, 1 cup	86	0.93
Milk, low-fat (1%), 1 cup	102	0.90
Cottage cheese, low-fat (1%), ½ cup	82	0.72
Tuna, fresh, cooked, 3 oz	118	0.51
Swiss cheese, 1 oz	107	0.48
Parmesan cheese, 1 oz	129	0.40
Lean ground turkey, cooked, 3 oz	169	0.39
Turkey breast, cooked, 3 oz	115	0.33
Turkey, dark meat, cooked, 3 oz	159	0.31
Chicken breast, cooked, 3 oz	140	0.29
Salmon, canned, 3 oz	130	0.26
Cheddar cheese, 1 oz	114	0.23
Mozzarella cheese, part-skim, 1 oz	72	0.23

vitamin B_6

food	calories	vitamin B_6 (mg)
Tuna, fresh, cooked, 3 oz	118	0.88
Baked potato, with skin, 1 large	220	0.70
Banana, 1 medium	109	0.68
Prune juice, 1 cup	182	0.56
Salmon fillet, cooked, 3 oz	175	0.55
Carrot juice, 1 cup	94	0.51
Chicken breast, cooked, 3 oz	140	0.51
Turkey breast, cooked, 3 oz	115	0.48
Green bell pepper, 1 large	44	0.41
Sweet potato, mashed, ½ cup	172	0.40
Snapper fillet, cooked, 3 oz	109	0.39
Pork tenderloin, cooked, 3 oz	139	0.36
Beef sirloin, cooked, 3 oz	170	0.33
Red bell pepper, 1 medium	32	0.30
Hass avocado, ½ medium	153	0.24
Chick-peas, cooked, 1 cup	269	0.23
Sunflower seeds, 1 oz	162	0.22
Pumpkin puree, canned, 1 cup	83	0.14

The charts below provide the adult RDAs established by the National Academy of Sciences for vitamins and minerals. For some vitamins and minerals, not enough is known to recommend a specific amount; in these cases, the Academy has recommended a range called the Estimated Safe and Adequate Daily Dietary Intake. All values are for adults (over age 19).

vitamins

Vitamin A	
women	700 mcg
men	900 mcg
Vitamin C	
women	75 mg
men	90 mg
Vitamin D	
age 19-50	200 IU
age 51-70	400 IU
age 70+	600 IU
Vitamin E	15 mg
Vitamin K	
women	90 mcg
men	120 mcg
Thiamin	
women	1.1 mg
men	1.2 mg
Riboflavin	
women	1.1 mg
men	1.3 mg
Niacin	
women	14 mg
men	16 mg
Pantothenic acid	5 mg
Vitamin B_6	
women and men 19-50	1.3 mg
women 51+	1.5 mg
men 51+	1.7 mg
Vitamin B_{12}	2.4 mcg
Folate (folic acid)	400 mcg
Biotin	30 mcg

minerals

Calcium	
age 19-50	1,000 mg
age 51+	1,200 mg
Chloride	No RDA
Chromium	
women 19-50	25 mcg
women 51+	20 mcg
men 19-50	35 mcg
men 51+	30 mcg
Copper	900 mcg
Fluoride	
women	3 mg
men	4 mg
Iodine	150 mcg
Iron	
women 19-50	18 mg
women 51+	8 mg
men 19+	8 mg
Magnesium	
women 19-30	310 mg
women 31+	320 mg
men 19-30	400 mg
men 31+	420 mg
Manganese	
women	1.8 mg
men	2.3 mg
Molybdenum	45 mcg
Phosphorus	700 mg
Potassium	1,600 to 2,000 mg minimum
Selenium	55 mcg
Sodium	2,400 mg maximum
Zinc	
women	8 mg
men	11 mg

A

Almonds
Apple & Date Crisp, 133
Country Captain, 75
Angel Food Cake, Chocolate-Flecked, 123
Appetizers
Caramelized Onion & Apple Focaccia, 24
Chinese Dumplings, 22
Curried White Bean Dip, 18
Fat-Free Black Bean Dip, 18
Portobello "Pizzas," 20
Salmon & Dill Pita Pizzas, 23
Sesame-Ginger Tofu, 21
Spicy Italian Chips, 19
Spicy Mexican Chips, 19
Tofu Salmon Spread, 145
Tuna & Basil Pita Pizzas, 23
Apples
Apple & Date Crisp, 133
Apple-Apricot Pie, 127
Apple-Cranberry Sauce, 128
Baked Apples with Date-Nut Stuffing, 122
Beet, Apple & Fennel Salad, 118
Caramelized Onion & Apple Focaccia, 24
Cream of Sweet Potato-Apple Soup, 28
Garlicky Sweet Potato & Apple Soup, 28
Lentil, Chick-Pea & Apple Salad, 117
Michel Nischan's Root Vegetable & Apple Gratin, 105
Pineapple-Broiled Chicken & Apple Salad, 72
Roasted Sweet Potato, Apple & Onion Salad, 116
Apricot, Apple-, Pie, 127
Asparagus
Asparagus & Lentil Salad with Tomato-Lemon Dressing, 121
Asparagus & Potatoes Vinaigrette, 119
Asparagus Vinaigrette, 119
Chicken Stir-Fry with Shiitake & Asparagus, 39
Shrimp Stir-Fry with Shiitake & Asparagus, 39

B

Banana-Peanut Smoothie, 140
Barbecued Pork & Mashed Sweet Potatoes, 59

Barley
Barley Pilaf with Apricots & Pistachios, 100
Carrot-Barley Soup, 35
Beans, dried or canned
Bean & Potato Salad with Mozzarella, 87
Black Bean & Corn Tortilla Soup, 33
Cannellini Beans with Rosemary & Parmesan, 99
Cannellini-Tomato Soup, 99
Chili Beans & Peppers, 108
Curried White Bean Dip, 18
Dilled White Bean & Potato Salad, 87
Fat-Free Black Bean Dip, 18
Mexican Pork & Beans, 57
No-Pork Baked Beans, 115
Peppered Tuna with Plum Tomato & Cannellini Salad, 37
Pork & Beans, 57
Rice & Beans Deluxe, 94
Vegetarian Chili, 86
Beef
Beef, Shiitake & Pasta Stir-Fry, 58
Heart-Smart Meatloaf, 54
Picadillo with Lentils, 55
Southwestern Beef Hash, 60
Southwestern Red Flannel Hash, 60
Beets
Beet, Apple & Fennel Salad, 118
Beet, Pear & Endive Salad, 118
Southwestern Red Flannel Hash, 60
Black beans
Black Bean & Corn Tortilla Soup, 33
Fat-Free Black Bean Dip, 18
Bluefish with Spicy Vegetable Sauce, 48
Bread Pudding, Apple-Raisin, 143
Bread. *See also Muffins*
Caramelized Onion & Apple Focaccia, 24
Dried Fruit & Bran Bread, 144
Whole-Wheat Walnut-Raisin Bread, 146
Breakfast/brunch
Apple-Raisin Bread Pudding, 143
Banana-Peanut Smoothie, 140
Breakfast Fruit Sundaes, 141
Buttermilk Waffles with Apple-Raisin Topping, 136
Corn & Egg Burritos, 139
Dried Fruit & Bran Bread, 144
Dried Plum & Toasted Oat Muffins, 147

Pineapple-Peach Smoothie, 140
Raspberry Whole-Grain Pancakes, 142
Shiitake-Tofu Scramble, 137
Super Heart-Smart Müesli Mix, 138
Tangerine Smoothie, 140
Tofu Salmon Spread, 145
Whole-Wheat Walnut-Raisin Bread, 146
Broccoli
Chicken, Broccoli & Porcini with Fettuccine, 66
Chunky Potato, Mushroom & Broccoli Soup, 25
Broth
Chicken Broth, 32
Garlic Broth, 32
Roasted Vegetable Broth, 32
Burgers
Broiled Salmon Burgers, 50
Broiled Tuna Burgers, 50
Indian-Style Turkey Burgers, 67
Shiitake Mushroom Burgers, 83
Burritos, Corn & Egg, 139
Buttermilk Waffles with Apple-Raisin Topping, 136
Butternut squash
Butternut Squash & Caramelized Onions, 109
Cheese Tortellini with Butternut-Marinara Sauce, 109

C

Cabbage
Colcannon, 104
Cabbage & Green Pepper Salad, 120
Pickled Pepper & Cabbage Salad, 120
Salmon with Braised Potatoes & Greens, 44
Stir-Fried Red Vegetables & Chicken, 76
Cakes
Chocolate-Flecked Angel Food Cake, 123
Chocolate-Raspberry Buttermilk Cupcakes, 130
Pumpkin Cheesecake with Oat-Walnut Crust, 134
Cannellini beans
Cannellini Beans with Rosemary & Parmesan, 99
Cannellini-Tomato Soup, 99
Curried White Bean Dip, 18
No-Pork Baked Beans, 115

Recipes for a Healthy Heart

recipe index

Cannellini beans continued
 Peppered Tuna with Plum Tomato & Cannellini Salad, 37

Carrots
 Baked Spiced Carrot Pudding, 126
 Carrot-Barley Soup, 35
 Curried Red Lentil-Carrot Soup, 29
 Gingered Carrot Soup, 35
 Golden Mashed Root Vegetables, 113
 Spiced Glazed Carrots, 111

Cereal
 Super Heart-Smart Müesli Mix, 138

Cheesecake, Pumpkin, with Oat-Walnut Crust, 134

Cherries
 Rhubarb-Cherry Compote, 125
 Wild & Brown Rice with Cherries & Walnuts, 103

Chick-peas
 Chick-Peas & Red Peppers, 108
 Lentil, Chick-Pea & Apple Salad, 117
 Moroccan Turkey & Chick-Pea Stew, 78
 Turkey, Chick-Pea & Corn Chili, 78

Chicken
 Broiled Chicken & Macaroni Salad, 65
 Broiled Chicken & Rice Salad, 72
 Chicken, Broccoli & Porcini with Fettuccine, 66
 Chicken Broth, 32
 Chicken Caesar, 62
 Chicken Chow Mein, 73
 Chicken & Corn Tortilla Soup, 33
 Chicken Kebabs with Minted Yogurt Sauce, 65
 Chicken Normandy, 69
 Chicken Salad with Golden Kiwi & Jícama, 68
 Chicken Salad with Kiwi & Honey-Lime Dressing, 68
 Chicken & Shiitake Mushrooms en Papillote, 77
 Chicken Stew with Peas & Mushrooms, 71
 Chicken Stir-Fry with Shiitake & Asparagus, 39
 Chicken with Red Wine & Dried Plums, 74
 Country Captain, 75
 Crispy Deviled Chicken, 62
 Hawaiian Chicken, 69
 Moroccan-Style Chicken, 46
 Pineapple-Broiled Chicken & Apple Salad, 72

Potato Soup with Chicken & Green Chilies, 30
 Stir-Fried Chicken & Tofu, 81
 Stir-Fried Red Vegetables & Chicken, 76

Chili
 Green Chili with Pork & Hominy, 61
 Turkey, Chick-Pea & Corn Chili, 78
 Vegetarian Chili, 86

Chinese Dumplings, 22
Chinese Roast Pork Salad, 53
Chipotle-Garlic Marinade, 56

Chips
 Spicy Italian Chips, 19
 Spicy Mexican Chips, 19

Chocolate-Flecked Angel Food Cake, 123
Chocolate-Raspberry Buttermilk Cupcakes, 130
Chow Mein, Chicken, 73
Chowder, Manhattan-Style Fresh Salmon, 34
Cod in Carrot-Vegetable Sauce, 45
Colcannon, 104

Compote
 Rhubarb-Cherry Compote, 125
 Strawberry-Rhubarb Compote, 125

Cookies, Walnut Meringue, 129

Corn
 Chicken & Corn Tortilla Soup, 33
 Corn & Egg Burritos, 139
 Turkey, Chick-Pea & Corn Chili, 78

Country Captain, 75
Cranberry, Apple-, Sauce, 128
Cream of Sweet Potato-Apple Soup, 28
"Cream" of Tomato-Basil Soup, 27
Creamy Almond Rice Pudding, 124
Creamy Basil-Lentil Soup, 36
Creamy Basil-Pea Soup, 36
Crème Brûlée, Pumpkin, 132
Crisp, Apple & Date, 133
Crispy Deviled Chicken, 62
Crunchy Baked Potato "Chips," 107
Cupcakes, Chocolate-Raspberry Buttermilk, 130

D

Date, Apple &, Crisp, 133
Desserts. *See also Cakes; Cookies; Pies*
 Apple & Date Crisp, 133
 Apple-Cranberry Sauce, 128
 Baked Apples with Date-Nut Stuffing, 122
 Baked Spiced Carrot Pudding, 126
 Creamy Almond Rice Pudding, 124

Fresh Grape Gelatin, 131
 Pumpkin Crème Brûlée, 132
 Rhubarb-Cherry Compote, 125
 Strawberry-Rhubarb Compote, 125
 Wine-Poached Plums with Yogurt Cream, 135

Dilled White Bean & Potato Salad, 87

Dips
 Curried White Bean Dip, 18
 Fat-Free Black Bean Dip, 18

Dumplings
 Baked Potato-Mozzarella Dumplings, 82
 Chinese Dumplings, 22

E-F

Eggs
 Corn & Egg Burritos, 139
 Shiitake-Tofu Scramble, 137

Fat-Free Black Bean Dip, 18

Fennel
 Beet, Apple & Fennel Salad, 118
 Quinoa with Fennel, Raisins & Parmesan, 88

Fish. *See also specific types*
 Baked Fish Fillets with Oat & Nut Crust, 51
 Bluefish with Spicy Vegetable Sauce, 48
 Broiled Salmon Burgers, 50
 Broiled Tuna Burgers, 50
 Cod in Carrot-Vegetable Sauce, 45
 Lemon-Broiled Snapper, 52
 Manhattan-Style Fresh Salmon Chowder, 34
 Moroccan-Style Fish Steaks, 46
 Orange-Broiled Snapper, 52
 Orange-Ginger Salmon, 38
 Parmesan Fish Sticks, 40
 Peppered Tuna with Plum Tomato & Cannellini Salad, 37
 Pineapple-Ginger Salmon, 38
 Salmon en Papillote, 49
 Salmon with Braised Potatoes & Greens, 44
 Salmon-Potato Loaf, 47
 Tandoori Salmon, 41

Flaxseeds
 Buttermilk Waffles with Apple-Raisin Topping, 136
 Raspberry Whole-Grain Pancakes, 142

Focaccia, Caramelized Onion & Apple, 24

Fruit
 Apple & Date Crisp, 133

Apple-Cranberry Sauce, 128
Baked Apples with Date-Nut Stuffing, 122
Breakfast Fruit Sundaes, 141
Dried Fruit & Bran Bread, 144
Fresh Grape Gelatin, 131
Rhubarb-Cherry Compote, 125
Strawberry-Rhubarb Compote, 125
Wine-Poached Plums with Yogurt Cream, 135

G
Garlic
Chipotle-Garlic Marinade, 56
Garlic Broth, 32
Garlicky Sweet Potato & Apple Soup, 28
Gelatin, Fresh Grape, 131
Ginger
Gingered Carrot Soup, 35
Pineapple-Ginger Marinade, 56
Grains. *See also Oats; Rice*
Barley Pilaf with Apricots & Pistachios, 100
Brown Rice & Wild Mushroom Pilaf, 98
Chilied Brown Rice, 101
Quinoa with Fennel, Raisins & Parmesan, 88
Raspberry Whole-Grain Pancakes, 142
Super Heart-Smart Müesli Mix, 138
Three-Pepper Rice, 101
Whole-Wheat Walnut-Raisin Bread, 146
Wild & Brown Rice with Cherries & Walnuts, 103
Grape, Fresh, Gelatin, 131
Greens, Salmon with Braised Potatoes &, 44

H
Hash. *See also Picadillo*
Southwestern Beef Hash, 60
Southwestern Red Flannel Hash, 60
Hominy, Green Chili with Pork &, 61

J-K
Jícama, Chicken Salad with Golden Kiwi &, 68
Kale
Salmon with Braised Potatoes & Greens, 44
Kebabs, Chicken, with Minted Yogurt Sauce, 65

Kiwifruit
Breakfast Fruit Sundaes, 141
Chicken Salad with Golden Kiwi & Jícama, 68
Chicken Salad with Kiwi & Honey-Lime Dressing, 68

L-M
Lentils
Asparagus & Lentil Salad with Tomato-Lemon Dressing, 121
Creamy Basil-Lentil Soup, 36
Curried Red Lentil-Carrot Soup, 29
Lentil, Chick-Pea & Apple Salad, 117
Lentil Vegetable Pilaf, 102
Picadillo with Lentils, 55
Vegetarian Picadillo, 55
Mac & Cheese, 91
Manhattan-Style Fresh Salmon Chowder, 34
Marinades
Chipotle-Garlic Marinade, 56
Pineapple-Ginger Marinade, 56
Thai-Style Marinade, 56
Meatballs
Asian Turkey Meatballs, 70
Basil-Tomato Turkey Meatballs, 70
Scallion-Mustard Turkey Meatballs, 70
Spaghetti & Basil-Tomato Meatballs, 80
Spaghetti with Chicken Meatballs, 80
Meatless main courses
All-Vegetable Pizza, 93
Baked Fusilli with Mushrooms, 84
Baked Potato-Mozzarella Dumplings, 82
Bean & Potato Salad with Mozzarella, 87
Brown Rice & Wild Mushroom Pilaf, 98
Chunky Potato, Mushroom & Broccoli Soup, 25
Cream of Sweet Potato-Apple Soup, 28
"Cream" of Tomato-Basil Soup, 27
Curried Mac & Cheese, 91
Curried Red Lentil-Carrot Soup, 29
Dilled White Bean & Potato Salad, 87
Garlicky Sweet Potato & Apple Soup, 28
Mac & Cheese, 91
Meatless Spaghetti Bolognese, 96
Mexican-Style Vegetarian Pizza, 93
Penne Salad with Pecan Pesto, 92
Pumpkin Couscous Risotto, 97
Pumpkin Lime Soup, 31

Quinoa with Fennel, Raisins & Parmesan, 88
Rice & Beans Deluxe, 94
Shiitake Mushroom Burgers, 83
Spicy Tortilla-Vegetable Casserole, 85
Thai Noodles with Tofu, 90
Tofu & Red Pepper Stir-Fry, 89
Vegetable Curry, 95
Vegetarian Chili, 86
Vegetarian Orzo Soup, 26
Vegetarian Picadillo, 55
Winter Squash & Lemon Soup, 31
Meatloaf
Extra-Moist Turkey Loaf, 79
Heart-Smart Meatloaf, 54
Meringue Cookies, Walnut, 129
Müesli Mix, Super Heart-Smart, 138
Muffins, Dried Plum & Toasted Oat, 147
Mushrooms
Baked Fusilli with Mushrooms, 84
Beef, Shiitake & Pasta Stir-Fry, 58
Brown Rice & Wild Mushroom Pilaf, 98
Chicken, Broccoli & Porcini with Fettuccine, 66
Chicken & Shiitake Mushrooms en Papillote, 77
Chicken Stew with Peas & Mushrooms, 71
Chicken Stir-Fry with Shiitake & Asparagus, 39
Chunky Potato, Mushroom & Broccoli Soup, 25
Mushroom-Pesto Mashed Potatoes, 110
Portobello "Pizzas," 20
Shiitake Mushroom Burgers, 83
Shiitake-Tofu Scramble, 137
Shrimp Stir-Fry with Shiitake & Asparagus, 39

N-O
Nischan, Michel
Root Vegetable & Apple Gratin, 105
Oats
Dried Plum & Toasted Oat Muffins, 147
Super Heart-Smart Müesli Mix, 138
Onions
Butternut Squash & Caramelized Onions, 109
Caramelized Onion & Apple Focaccia, 24
Roasted Sweet Potato, Apple & Onion Salad, 116

Recipes for a Healthy Heart

recipe index

P

Pancakes, Raspberry Whole-Grain, 142

Parsnips
Michel Nischan's Root Vegetable & Apple Gratin, 105

Pasta
Baked Fusilli with Mushrooms, 84
Baked Potato-Mozzarella Dumplings, 82
Broiled Chicken & Macaroni Salad, 65
Cheese Tortellini with Butternut-Marinara Sauce, 109
Chicken, Broccoli & Porcini with Fettuccine, 66
Chicken Chow Mein, 73
Curried Mac & Cheese, 91
Mac & Cheese, 91
Meatless Spaghetti Bolognese, 96
Penne Salad with Pecan Pesto, 92
Pumpkin Couscous Risotto, 97
Rosemary Shrimp Pasta Sauce, 42
Spaghetti & Basil-Tomato Meatballs, 80
Spaghetti with Chicken Meatballs, 80
Thai Noodles with Tofu, 90

Pear, Beet, & Endive Salad, 118

Peas
Chicken Stew with Peas & Mushrooms, 71
Creamy Basil-Pea Soup, 36
Two-Pea Sauté, 112

Pecan Pesto, Penne Salad with, 92

Peppers, bell
Cabbage & Green Pepper Salad, 120
Chick-Peas & Red Peppers, 108
Chili Beans & Peppers, 108
Pickled Pepper & Cabbage Salad, 120
Three-Pepper Rice, 101
Tofu & Red Pepper Stir-Fry, 89

Picadillo
Picadillo with Lentils, 55
Vegetarian Picadillo, 55

Pie, Apple-Apricot, 127

Pilaf
Barley Pilaf with Apricots & Pistachios, 100
Brown Rice & Wild Mushroom Pilaf, 98
Lentil Vegetable Pilaf, 102

Pineapple
Pineapple-Broiled Chicken & Apple Salad, 72
Pineapple-Ginger Marinade, 56
Pineapple-Peach Smoothie, 140

Pizza. *See also Focaccia*
All-Vegetable Pizza, 93
Mexican-Style Vegetarian Pizza, 93
Portobello "Pizzas," 20
Salmon & Dill Pita Pizzas, 23
Tuna & Basil Pita Pizzas, 23

Plums, dried (prunes)
Chicken with Red Wine & Dried Plums, 74
Dried Plum & Toasted Oat Muffins, 147

Plums, fresh
Breakfast Fruit Sundaes, 141
Wine-Poached Plums with Yogurt Cream, 135

Pork
Barbecued Pork & Mashed Sweet Potatoes, 59
Chinese Roast Pork Salad, 53
Green Chili with Pork & Hominy, 61
Mexican Pork & Beans, 57
Pork & Beans, 57

Portobello "Pizzas," 20

Potatoes
Asparagus & Potatoes Vinaigrette, 119
Baked Potato-Mozzarella Dumplings, 82
Bean & Potato Salad with Mozzarella, 87
Cheese-Stuffed Potatoes with Fresh Salsa, 114
Chunky Potato, Mushroom & Broccoli Soup, 25
Colcannon, 104
Crunchy Baked Potato "Chips," 107
Dilled White Bean & Potato Salad, 87
Golden Mashed Root Vegetables, 113
Michel Nischan's Root Vegetable & Apple Gratin, 105
Mushroom-Pesto Mashed Potatoes, 110
Potato Soup with Chicken & Green Chilies, 30
Salmon with Braised Potatoes & Greens, 44

Prunes. *See Plums, dried*

Pudding
Apple-Raisin Bread Pudding, 143
Baked Spiced Carrot Pudding, 126
Creamy Almond Rice Pudding, 124
Pumpkin Crème Brûlée, 132

Pumpkin
Pumpkin Cheesecake with Oat-Walnut Crust, 134

Pumpkin Couscous Risotto, 97
Pumpkin Crème Brûlée, 132
Pumpkin Lime Soup, 31

Q-R

Quinoa with Fennel, Raisins & Parmesan, 88

Raspberry Whole-Grain Pancakes, 142

Rhubarb
Rhubarb-Cherry Compote, 125
Strawberry-Rhubarb Compote, 125

Rice
Broiled Chicken & Rice Salad, 72
Brown Rice & Wild Mushroom Pilaf, 98
Chilied Brown Rice, 101
Creamy Almond Rice Pudding, 124
Rice & Beans Deluxe, 94
Stir-Fried Italian Rice & Vegetables, 106
Three-Pepper Rice, 101
Wild & Brown Rice with Cherries & Walnuts, 103

S

Salads, main-course
Bean & Potato Salad with Mozzarella, 87
Broiled Chicken & Macaroni Salad, 65
Broiled Chicken & Rice Salad, 72
Chicken Caesar, 62
Chicken Salad with Golden Kiwi & Jícama, 68
Chicken Salad with Kiwi & Honey-Lime Dressing, 68
Chinese Roast Pork Salad, 53
Curried Smoked Turkey Salad, 64
Dilled White Bean & Potato Salad, 87
Penne Salad with Pecan Pesto, 92
Peppered Tuna with Plum Tomato & Cannellini Salad, 37
Pineapple-Broiled Chicken & Apple Salad, 72

Salads, side-dish
Asparagus & Lentil Salad with Tomato-Lemon Dressing, 121
Asparagus & Potatoes Vinaigrette, 119
Asparagus Vinaigrette, 119
Beet, Apple & Fennel Salad, 118
Beet, Pear & Endive Salad, 118
Cabbage & Green Pepper Salad, 120
Lentil, Chick-Pea & Apple Salad, 117
Pickled Pepper & Cabbage Salad, 120

Roasted Sweet Potato, Apple & Onion Salad, 116
Salmon. *See also Smoked salmon*
    Broiled Salmon Burgers, 50
    Manhattan-Style Fresh Salmon Chowder, 34
    Orange-Ginger Salmon, 38
    Pineapple-Ginger Salmon, 38
    Salmon & Dill Pita Pizzas, 23
    Salmon en Papillote, 49
    Salmon with Braised Potatoes & Greens, 44
    Salmon-Potato Loaf, 47
    Tandoori Salmon, 41
Sauces, savory. *See also Marinades*
    Balsamic-Ketchup Dipping Sauce, 43
    Honey-Mustard Dipping Sauce, 43
    Lemon-Herb Dipping Sauce, 43
Scallops in Carrot-Vegetable Sauce, 45
Shrimp
    Herb-Grilled Shrimp, 42
    Rosemary Shrimp Pasta Sauce, 42
    Shrimp Stir-Fry with Shiitake & Asparagus, 39
Smoked salmon
    Tofu Salmon Spread, 145
Smoothies
    Banana-Peanut Smoothie, 140
    Pineapple-Peach Smoothie, 140
    Tangerine Smoothie, 140
Snapper
    Lemon-Broiled Snapper, 52
    Orange-Broiled Snapper, 52
Soups. *See also Broth*
    Black Bean & Corn Tortilla Soup, 33
    Cannellini-Tomato Soup, 99
    Carrot-Barley Soup, 35
    Chicken & Corn Tortilla Soup, 33
    Chunky Potato, Mushroom & Broccoli Soup, 25
    Cream of Sweet Potato-Apple Soup, 28
    "Cream" of Tomato-Basil Soup, 27
    Creamy Basil-Lentil Soup, 36
    Creamy Basil-Pea Soup, 36
    Curried Red Lentil-Carrot Soup, 29
    Garlicky Sweet Potato & Apple Soup, 28
    Gingered Carrot Soup, 35
    Greek Orzo-Vegetable Soup, 26
    Manhattan-Style Fresh Salmon Chowder, 34
    Potato Soup with Chicken & Green Chilies, 30

Pumpkin Lime Soup, 31
Vegetarian Orzo Soup, 26
Winter Squash & Lemon Soup, 31
Squash, winter
    Butternut Squash & Caramelized Onions, 109
    Cheese Tortellini with Butternut-Marinara Sauce, 109
    Spicy Tortilla-Vegetable Casserole, 85
    Winter Squash & Lemon Soup, 31
Stews
    Chicken Stew with Peas & Mushrooms, 71
    Country Captain, 75
    Green Chili with Pork & Hominy, 61
    Moroccan Turkey & Chick-Pea Stew, 78
    Turkey, Chick-Pea & Corn Chili, 78
    Vegetarian Chili, 86
Strawberries
    Breakfast Fruit Sundaes, 141
    Strawberry-Rhubarb Compote, 125
Sweet potatoes
    Barbecued Pork & Mashed Sweet Potatoes, 59
    Cream of Sweet Potato-Apple Soup, 28
    Garlicky Sweet Potato & Apple Soup, 28
    Golden Mashed Root Vegetables, 113
    Michel Nischan's Root Vegetable & Apple Gratin, 105
    Roasted Sweet Potato, Apple & Onion Salad, 116

T
Tangerine Smoothie, 140
Tetrazzini, Turkey , 63
Tofu
    "Cream" of Tomato-Basil Soup, 27
    Sesame-Ginger Tofu, 21
    Shiitake-Tofu Scramble, 137
    Stir-Fried Chicken & Tofu, 81
    Thai Noodles with Tofu, 90
    Tofu & Red Pepper Stir-Fry, 89
    Tofu Salmon Spread, 145
Tomato-Basil Soup, "Cream" of, 27
Tortellini, Cheese, with Butternut-Marinara Sauce, 109
Tortillas
    Black Bean & Corn Tortilla Soup, 33
    Chicken & Corn Tortilla Soup, 33
    Spicy Tortilla-Vegetable Casserole, 85
Tuna
    Broiled Tuna Burgers, 50

Peppered Tuna with Plum Tomato & Cannellini Salad, 37
Tuna & Basil Pita Pizzas, 23
Turkey
    Asian Turkey Meatballs, 70
    Basil-Tomato Turkey Meatballs, 70
    Curried Smoked Turkey Salad, 64
    Extra-Moist Turkey Loaf, 79
    Heart-Smart Meatloaf, 54
    Indian-Style Turkey Burgers, 67
    Moroccan Turkey & Chick-Pea Stew, 78
    Scallion-Mustard Turkey Meatballs, 70
    Turkey, Chick-Pea & Corn Chili, 78
    Turkey Tetrazzini, 63
Turnips
    Golden Mashed Root Vegetables, 113

V
Vegetable main dishes. *See Meatless main courses*
Vegetable side dishes. *See also specific vegetables*
    Butternut Squash & Caramelized Onions, 109
    Cannellini Beans with Rosemary & Parmesan, 99
    Cheese-Stuffed Potatoes with Fresh Salsa, 114
    Chick-Peas & Red Peppers, 108
    Chili Beans & Peppers, 108
    Colcannon, 104
    Crunchy Baked Potato "Chips," 107
    Golden Mashed Root Vegetables, 113
    Lentil Vegetable Pilaf, 102
    Michel Nischan's Root Vegetable & Apple Gratin, 105
    Mushroom-Pesto Mashed Potatoes, 110
    No-Pork Baked Beans, 115
    Spiced Glazed Carrots, 111
    Stir-Fried Italian Rice & Vegetables, 106
    Two-Pea Sauté, 112

W
Waffles, Buttermilk, with Apple-Raisin Topping, 136
Walnuts
    Walnut Meringue Cookies, 129
    Whole-Wheat Walnut-Raisin Bread, 146
Wild & Brown Rice with Cherries & Walnuts, 103

Recipes for a Healthy Heart

SIMEON MARGOLIS, M.D., PH.D., received his B.A., M.D., and Ph.D. from the Johns Hopkins University School of Medicine and performed his internship and residency at Johns Hopkins Hospital. He is currently a professor of medicine and biological chemistry at the Johns Hopkins University School of Medicine and medical editor of *The Johns Hopkins Medical Letter: Health After 50*. Dr. Margolis is also the consulting medical editor for *The Johns Hopkins Cookbook Library*. He has served on various committees for the Department of Health, Education and Welfare, including the National Diabetes Advisory Board and the Arteriosclerosis Specialized Centers of Research Review Committees. In addition, he has acted as a member of the Endocrinology and Metabolism Panel of the U.S. Food and Drug Administration.

A former weekly columnist for the *Baltimore Sun*, Dr. Margolis lectures regularly to medical students, physicians, and the general public on a wide variety of topics, such as the prevention of coronary heart disease, controlling cholesterol levels, the treatment of diabetes, and alternative medicine.

LORA BROWN WILDER, SC.D., M.S., R.D., a registered dietitian, received her M.S. in nutrition from the University of Maryland and her Sc.D. in public health from Johns Hopkins University. She is currently an assistant professor at the Johns Hopkins School of Medicine, and is also affiliated with the USDA and the University of Maryland's Department of Nutrition and Food Science. Dr. Wilder has served on various advisory committees related to nutrition, including the American Heart Association and the National Institutes of Health, and helped set up the first Johns Hopkins Preventive Cardiology Program.

In her research, Dr. Wilder has studied the effects of coffee on fatty acids and investigated behavioral strategies to reduce coronary risk factors. Her current research is in the area of dietary assessment methodology. She contributed to *Nutritional Management: The Johns Hopkins Handbook* and has been published in such journals as *Circulation, American Journal of Medicine*, and *Journal of the American Medical Association*.

The Johns Hopkins Cookbook Library is published by Medletter Associates, Inc.

Rodney Friedman Publisher

Kate Slate Executive Editor

Sandra Rose Gluck Test Kitchen Director, Food Editor

Timothy Jeffs Art Director

Maureen Mulhern-White Senior Writer

Patricia Kaupas Writer/Researcher

James W. Brown Associate Editor